Learning Raspbian

Get up and running with Raspbian and make the most out of your Raspberry Pi

William Harrington

BIRMINGHAM - MUMBAI

Learning Raspbian

First published: February 2015

Production reference: 1190215

Published by Packt Publishing Ltd.
Livery Place
35 Livery Street
Birmingham B3 2PB, UK.

ISBN 978-1-78439-219-2

www.packtpub.com

Cover image by William Harrington (william@usee.com.au)

Credits

Author
William Harrington

Reviewers
Robin David
Özen Özkaya
Nicola Pisanti

Commissioning Editor
Amarabha Banerjee

Acquisition Editor
Neha Nagwekar

Content Development Editor
Ritika Singh

Technical Editor
Mitali Somaiya

Copy Editors
Dipti Kapadia
Vikrant Phadke
Rashmi Sawant

Project Coordinator
Aboli Ambardekar

Proofreaders
Simran Bhogal
Safis Editing
Paul Hindle

Indexer
Rekha Nair

Graphics
Sheetal Aute

Production Coordinator
Komal Ramchandani

Cover Work
Komal Ramchandani

About the Author

William Harrington lives and works at his family's cattle station, Olga Downs, in northwest Queensland, Australia. He attended university at James Cook University, Townsville. At the age of 20, he established his own company, Harrington Systems Electronics, which sells the NLIS RFID tag reader – The Pipe Reader that he designed and manufactures. He also received the AgForce President's Innovation Award in 2005. In 2006, he graduated with honors as a computer systems engineer and received the Queensland Primary Industries Young Achiever Award. Since then, he has gone on to design the uSee remote monitoring system, a revolutionary and low-cost remote monitoring solution.

Having a home-based company has become part of a unique diversification strategy for the family and has provided them the opportunity to stay on the land. Due to a never-ending passion for technology, William speaks regularly on many topics, so he will bring a futuristic version of the technology that is possible in the next decade.

Since 2011, he has also been a director and programmer for Farm Apps Pty Ltd, developing smartphone and tablet apps that increase farming efficiency.

He enjoys travelling and brewing beer at home.

William works alongside his wife Hollie, having recently welcomed their young son, Jack, into the world.

I would like to thank my wife, Hollie, for her love and support throughout the process of writing this book. I would also like to thank our son, Jack, for reminding us that he is there, along with the rest of my family, Peter, Carmel, Emily, and Grace!

About the Reviewers

Robin David is a technology enthusiast who is passionate about computer security and electronics. His background in computer science and his experience in Linux administration, especially Debian, inevitably led him to use Raspbian as the operating system for Raspberry-Pi-related projects. From his point of view, the Raspberry Pi is currently the best prototyping platform, which brings new perspectives to experimenting and creating small and lightweight projects at a low cost.

That's why he was glad to participate in the review of this book, which is a great introduction to Raspbian for any newcomers to the Linux ecosystem and the Raspberry Pi world.

His Twitter handle is `@RobinDavid1` or you can reach him via e-mail at `mail.robin.david@gmail.com`.

> I would to thank everyone participating in the Raspberry Pi community and more generally, all the people who encourage open source initiatives as well as share ideas, projects, and efforts in order to make the Internet a better and safer place.

Özen Özkaya is an embedded systems engineer who has been involved in the design, development, and verification of various kinds of embedded systems for more than 6 years now. His skills are not limited to embedded systems. He has a deep knowledge of computer vision, cryptography, software quality, machine learning, and the Internet of Things. He strongly believes in the power of sharing knowledge and continuously extending the vision.

After 6 years of experience in the profession, he is now working for Siemens as a senior development engineer, where he is involved in the research and development of industrial control devices and industrial communication processors. He also contributes to software quality assurance projects at Siemens. He has a total of eight patent applications, and all of his applications are still in progress.

He has a bachelor's degree in electronics engineering from Istanbul Technical University (ITU) with high honor certificates. He holds a master's degree in electronics engineering from ITU, and he is currently a PhD candidate in electronics engineering at ITU. As a part of his academic studies, he worked in various laboratories, such as a medical system design lab, a control and avionics lab, a robotics lab, a pattern recognition and signal processing lab, an industrial automation lab, and lastly, embedded systems lab. He is also a mentor in the embedded systems lab. At ITU, he is currently working on security and privacy in the Internet of Things for his PhD thesis.

Özen can be reached directly via e-mail at ozenozkaya@gmail.com or contact@ozenozkaya.com. If you want to learn more about him, you can visit his website, http://www.ozenozkaya.com. He is also a blog writer and his blog is http://www.ozenozkaya.com/blog/.

First, I would like to thank my parents, Kıyas and Ferah, for their endless effort and perseverance in bringing me up to this level. My academic advisor associate professor Dr. S. Berna Örs Yalcin has always supported me and helped me a lot to achieve many things, so I would like to thank her. I would also like to thank all my friends; the list is too long to mention here.

Above all, a huge and special thanks to Nilay Tüfek for helping me a lot in reviewing this book. She also encouraged me to accept this challenge and succeed at it.

Congratulations to the author and all those who worked on this book. Also, thanks to the editors and publishers, who gave me a chance to work on the review of this book.

Nicola Pisanti is a creative technologist who works on audiovisual artistic installations and digital musical instrument design and implementation. He always tries to merge different skills and concepts acquired while studying and working in many different fields, such as creative coding, soundtrack creation, sound design, and improvised musical instrument craft. You can find out more about him at www.npisanti.com.

www.PacktPub.com

Support files, eBooks, discount offers, and more

For support files and downloads related to your book, please visit www.PacktPub.com.

Did you know that Packt offers eBook versions of every book published, with PDF and ePub files available? You can upgrade to the eBook version at www.PacktPub.com and as a print book customer, you are entitled to a discount on the eBook copy. Get in touch with us at service@packtpub.com for more details.

At www.PacktPub.com, you can also read a collection of free technical articles, sign up for a range of free newsletters and receive exclusive discounts and offers on Packt books and eBooks.

https://www2.packtpub.com/books/subscription/packtlib

Do you need instant solutions to your IT questions? PacktLib is Packt's online digital book library. Here, you can search, access, and read Packt's entire library of books.

Why subscribe?

- Fully searchable across every book published by Packt
- Copy and paste, print, and bookmark content
- On demand and accessible via a web browser

Free access for Packt account holders

If you have an account with Packt at www.PacktPub.com, you can use this to access PacktLib today and view 9 entirely free books. Simply use your login credentials for immediate access.

Table of Contents

Preface

This book is an introduction to the revolutionary Raspberry Pi computer and its official operating system, Raspbian. Raspbian is a free, open source operating system based on the extremely popular Debian Linux distribution. Raspbian has been specifically customized for maximum performance on the Raspberry Pi.

After reading this book, you will be able to do the following:

- Set up and configure a Raspberry Pi from scratch
- Install and configure the Raspbian operating system
- Customize the desktop environment to suit your requirements and taste
- Install and manage software packages on your Raspberry Pi

You can get a good understanding of the capabilities of your Raspberry Pi and Raspbian by taking a look at some of the other projects that are based on Raspbian.

What this book covers

Chapter 1, *The Raspberry Pi and Raspbian*, runs you through the history of the Raspberry Pi and the different hardware and software components that make up the Raspberry Pi.

Chapter 2, *Getting Started with Raspbian*, walks you through how to set up your Raspberry Pi and how to load Raspbian onto your SD card.

Chapter 3, *Starting Raspbian*, walks you through the initial setup of Raspbian and the Linux boot process.

Chapter 4, *An Introduction to the Raspbian Desktop*, details the Raspbian desktop and runs you through the preinstalled software that is included with Raspbian.

Chapter 5, *Installing Software on Raspbian*, teaches you how to install software on your Raspberry Pi using the different methods explained in this chapter.

Chapter 6, The Console, takes you through the basic use of the bash console in Raspbian.

Chapter 7, Other Linux Distributions Based on Raspbian, looks at several other exciting projects that are based on Raspbian.

Appendix, References, lists a collection of links to the resources used in this book and other interesting information.

What you need for this book

You will need the following in order to work with the examples in this book:

- A Raspberry Pi
- A 4 GB or bigger SD card
- A USB keyboard and mouse
- A monitor (preferably with HDMI)
- An HDMI cable
- A micro USB phone charger as a power supply

All of these are available from element14. Don't forget to grab a cup of coffee!

Who this book is for

This book is written for beginners who wish to learn how to make the most out of their Raspberry Pi and learn more about Raspbian, the official Linux operating system for the Raspberry Pi.

Conventions

In this book, you will find a number of text styles that distinguish between different kinds of information. Here are some examples of these styles and an explanation of their meaning.

Code words in text, database table names, folder names, filenames, file extensions, pathnames, dummy URLs, user input, and Twitter handles are shown as follows: "It is a software tool that actually installs a software package from a `.deb` file."

Any command-line input or output is written as follows:

```
sudo apt-get install apache2
```

New terms and **important words** are shown in bold. Words that you see on the screen, for example, in menus or dialog boxes, appear in the text like this: "Simply select **Mark** and then click on **Apply**."

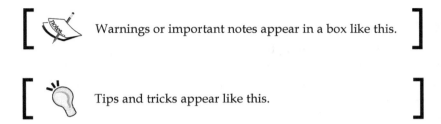

Warnings or important notes appear in a box like this.

Tips and tricks appear like this.

Reader feedback

Feedback from our readers is always welcome. Let us know what you think about this book—what you liked or disliked. Reader feedback is important for us as it helps us develop titles that you will really get the most out of.

To send us general feedback, simply e-mail feedback@packtpub.com, and mention the book's title in the subject of your message.

If there is a topic that you have expertise in and you are interested in either writing or contributing to a book, see our author guide at www.packtpub.com/authors.

Customer support

Now that you are the proud owner of a Packt book, we have a number of things to help you to get the most from your purchase.

Errata

Although we have taken every care to ensure the accuracy of our content, mistakes do happen. If you find a mistake in one of our books—maybe a mistake in the text or the code—we would be grateful if you could report this to us. By doing so, you can save other readers from frustration and help us improve subsequent versions of this book. If you find any errata, please report them by visiting http://www.packtpub.com/submit-errata, selecting your book, clicking on the **Errata Submission Form** link, and entering the details of your errata. Once your errata are verified, your submission will be accepted and the errata will be uploaded to our website or added to any list of existing errata under the Errata section of that title.

To view the previously submitted errata, go to https://www.packtpub.com/books/content/support and enter the name of the book in the search field. The required information will appear under the **Errata** section.

Piracy

Piracy of copyrighted material on the Internet is an ongoing problem across all media. At Packt, we take the protection of our copyright and licenses very seriously. If you come across any illegal copies of our works in any form on the Internet, please provide us with the location address or website name immediately so that we can pursue a remedy.

Please contact us at copyright@packtpub.com with a link to the suspected pirated material.

We appreciate your help in protecting our authors and our ability to bring you valuable content.

Questions

If you have a problem with any aspect of this book, you can contact us at questions@packtpub.com, and we will do our best to address the problem.

1
The Raspberry Pi and Raspbian

In this chapter, you will learn about the Raspberry Pi, the Raspberry Pi Foundation and Raspbian, the official Linux-based operating system of Raspberry Pi.

In this chapter, we will cover:

- The Raspberry Pi
- History of the Raspberry Pi
- The Raspberry Pi hardware
- The Raspbian operating system
- Raspbian components

The Raspberry Pi

Despite first impressions, the Raspberry Pi is not a tasty snack. The Raspberry Pi is a small, powerful, and inexpensive single board computer developed over several years by the Raspberry Pi Foundation.

If you are a looking for a low cost, small, easy-to-use computer for your next project, or are interested in learning how computers work, then the Raspberry Pi is for you.

The Raspberry Pi was designed as an educational device and was inspired by the success of the BBC Micro for teaching computer programming to a generation. The Raspberry Pi Foundation set out to do the same in today's world, where you don't need to know how to write software to use a computer. At the time of printing, the Raspberry Pi Foundation had shipped over *2.5 million* units, and it is safe to say that they have exceeded their expectations!

The Raspberry Pi Foundation

The Raspberry Pi Foundation is a not-for-profit charity and was founded in 2006 by Eben Upton, Rob Mullins, Jack Lang, and Alan Mycroft. The aim of this charity is to promote the study of computer science to a generation that didn't grow up with the BBC Micro or the Commodore 64.

They became concerned about the lack of devices that a hobbyist could use to learn and experiment with. The home computer was often ruled out, as it was so expensive, leaving the hobbyist and children with nothing to develop their skills with.

History of the Raspberry Pi

Any new product goes through many iterations before mass production. In the case of the Raspberry Pi, it all began in 2006 when several concept versions of the Raspberry Pi based on the Atmel 8-bit ATMega664 microcontroller were developed. Another concept based on a USB memory stick with an ARM processor (similar to what is used in the current Raspberry Pi) was created after that. It took six years of hardware development to create the Raspberry Pi that we know and love today!

The official logo of the Raspberry Pi is shown in the following screenshot:

It wasn't until August 2011 when 50 boards of the Alpha version of the Raspberry Pi were built. These boards were slightly larger than the current version to allow the Raspberry Pi Foundation, to debug the device and confirm that it would all work as expected. Twenty-five beta versions of the Raspberry Pi were assembled in December 2011 and auctioned to raise money for the Raspberry Pi Foundation. Only a single small error with these was found and corrected for the first production run.

The first production run consisted of 10,000 boards of Raspberry Pi manufactured overseas in China and Taiwan. Unfortunately, there was a problem with the Ethernet jack on the Raspberry Pi being incorrectly substituted with an incompatible part. This led to some minor shipping delays, but all the Raspberry Pi boards were delivered within weeks of their due date. As a bonus, the foundation was able to upgrade the Model A Raspberry Pi to 256 MB of RAM instead of the 128 MB that was planned. This upgrade in memory size allowed the Raspberry Pi to perform even more amazing tasks, such as real-time image processing.

The Raspberry Pi is now manufactured in the United Kingdom, leading to the creation of many new jobs.

The release of the Raspberry Pi was met with great fanfare, and the two original retailers of the Raspberry Pi - Premier Farnell and RS components-sold out of the first batch within minutes.

The Raspberry Pi hardware

At the heart of Raspberry Pi is the powerful Broadcom BCM2835 "system on a chip". The BCM2835 is similar to the chip at the heart of almost every smartphone and set top box in the world that uses ARM architecture. The BCM2835 CPU on the Raspberry Pi runs at 700 MHz and its performance is roughly equivalent to a 300 MHz Pentium II computer that was available back in 1999.

To put this in perspective, the guidance computer used in the Apollo missions was less powerful than a pocket calculator!

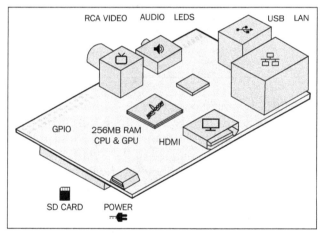

Block diagram of the Raspberry Pi

The Raspberry Pi comes with either 256 MB or 512 MB of RAM, depending on which model you buy. Hopefully, this will increase in future versions!

Graphic capabilities

Graphics in the Raspberry Pi are provided by a Videocore 4 GPU. The graphic performance of the **graphics processing unit (GPU)** is roughly equivalent to the Xbox, launched in 2011, which cost many hundreds of dollars. These might seem like very low specifications, but they are enough to play Quake 3 at 1080p and full HD movies.

There are two ways to connect a display to the Raspberry Pi. The first is using a composite video cable and the second is using HDMI. The composite output is useful as you are able to use any old TV as a monitor. The HDMI output is recommended however, as it provides superior video quality. A VGA connection is not provided on the Raspberry Pi as it would be cost prohibitive. However, it is possible to use an HDMI to VGA/DVI converter for users who have VGA or DVI monitors.

The Raspberry Pi also supports an LCD touchscreen. An official version has not been released yet, although many unofficial ones are available. The Raspberry Pi Foundation says that they expect to release one this year.

The Raspberry Pi model

The Raspberry Pi has several different variants: the Model A and the Model B. The Model A is a low-cost version and unfortunately omits the USB hub chip. This chip also functions as a USB to an Ethernet converter. The Raspberry Pi Foundation has also just released the Raspberry Pi Model B+ that has extra USB ports and resolves many of the power issues surrounding the Model B and Model B USB ports.

Parameters	Model A	Model B	Model B+
CPU	BCM2835	BCM2835	BCM2835
RAM	256 MB	512 MB	512 MB
USB Ports	1	2	4
Ethernet Ports	0	1	1
Price (USD)	~$25	~$35	~$35
Available since	February 2012	February 2012	July 2014
Boards			

Differences between the Raspberry Pi models

 Did you know that the Raspberry Pi is so popular that if you search for `raspberry pie` in Google, they will actually show you results for the Raspberry Pi!

Accessories

The success of the Raspberry Pi has encouraged many other groups to design accessories for the Raspberry Pi, and users to use them. These accessories range from a camera to a controller for an automatic CNC machine. Some of these accessories include:

Accessories	Links
Raspberry Pi camera	http://www.raspberrypi.org/tag/camera-board/
VGA board	http://www.suptronics.com/RPI.html
CNC Controller	http://code.google.com/p/picnc/
Autopilot	http://www.emlid.com/
Case	http://shortcrust.net/

Raspbian

No matter how good the hardware of the Raspberry Pi is, without an operating system it is just a piece of silicon, fiberglass, and a few other materials. There are several different operating systems for the Raspberry Pi, including RISC OS, Pidora, Arch Linux, and Raspbian.

Currently, Raspbian is the most popular Linux-based operating system for the Raspberry Pi. Raspbian is an open source operating system based on Debian, which has been modified specifically for the Raspberry Pi (thus the name Raspbian). Raspbian includes customizations that are designed to make the Raspberry Pi easier to use and includes many different software packages out of the box.

Raspbian is designed to be easy to use and is the recommended operating system for beginners to start off with their Raspberry Pi.

Debian

The Debian operating system was created in August 1993 by Ian Murdock and is one of the original distributions of Linux.

As Raspbian is based on the Debian operating system, it shares almost all the features of Debian, including its large repository of software packages. There are over 35,000 free software packages available for your Raspberry Pi, and they are available for use right now!

An excellent resource for more information on Debian, and therefore Raspbian, is the Debian administrator's handbook. The handbook is available at `http://debian-handbook.info`.

Open source software

The majority of the software that makes up Raspbian on the Raspberry Pi is open source. Open source software is a software whose source code is available for modification or enhancement by anyone.

The Linux kernel and most of the other software that makes up Raspbian is licensed under the GPLv2 License. This means that the software is made available to you at no cost, and that the source code that makes up the software is available for you to do what you want to. The GPLV2 license also removes any claim or warranty. The following extract from the GPLV2 license preamble gives you a good idea of the spirit of free software:

> *"The licenses for most software are designed to take away your freedom to share and change it. By contrast, the GNU General Public License is intended to guarantee your freedom to share and change free software--to make sure the software is free for all its users....*
>
> *When we speak of free software, we are referring to freedom, not price. Our General Public Licenses are designed to make sure that you have the freedom to distribute copies of free software (and charge for this service if you wish), that you receive source code or can get it if you want it, that you can change the software or use pieces of it in new free programs; and that you know you can do these things."*

Raspbian components

There are many components that make up a modern Linux distribution. These components work together to provide you with all the modern features you expect in a computer.

There are several key components that Raspbian is built from. These components are:

- The Raspberry Pi bootloader
- The Linux kernel
- Daemons
- The shell
- Shell utilities

- The X.Org graphical server
- The desktop environment

The Raspberry Pi bootloader

When your Raspberry Pi is powered on, lot of things happen behind the scene. The role of the bootloader is to initialize the hardware in the Raspberry Pi to a known state, and then to start loading the Linux kernel. In the case of the Raspberry Pi, this is done by the first and second stage bootloaders. The first stage bootloader is programmed into the ROM of the Raspberry Pi during manufacture and cannot be modified. The second and third stage bootloaders are stored on the SD card and are automatically run by the previous stage bootloader.

The Linux kernel

The Linux kernel is one of the most fundamental parts of Raspbian. It manages every part of the operation of your Raspberry Pi, from displaying text on the screen to receiving keystrokes when you type on your keyboard.

The Linux kernel was created by Linus Torvalds, who started working on the kernel in April 1991. Since then, groups of volunteers and organizations have worked together to continue the development of the kernel and make it what it is today.

 Did you know that the cost to rewrite the Linux kernel to where it was in 2011 would be over $3 billion USD?

The Linux logo is a penguin named Tux:

If you want to use a hardware device by connecting it to your Raspberry Pi, the kernel needs to know what it is and how to use it. The vast majority of devices on the market are supported by the Linux kernel, with more being added all the time. A good example of this is when you plug a USB drive into your Raspberry Pi. In this case, the kernel automatically detects the USB drive and notifies a daemon that automatically makes the files available to you.

When the kernel has finished loading, it automatically runs a program called init. This program is designed to finish the initialization of the Raspberry Pi, and then to load the rest of the operating system. This program starts by loading all the daemons into the background, followed by the graphical user interface.

Daemons

A daemon is a piece of software that runs behind the scenes to provide the operating system with different features. Some examples of a daemon include the Apache web server, Cron, a job scheduler that is used to run programs automatically at different times, and Autofs, a daemon that automatically mounts removable storage devices such as USB drives.

A distribution such as Raspbian needs more than just the kernel to work. It also needs other software that allows the user to interact with the kernel, and to manage the rest of the operating system. The core operating system consists of a collection of programs and scripts that make this happen.

The shell

After all the daemons have loaded, init launches a shell. A shell is an interface to your Raspberry Pi that allows you to monitor and control it using commands typed in using a keyboard. Don't be fooled by this interface, despite the fact that it looks exactly like what was used in computers 30 years ago. The shell is one of the most powerful parts of Raspbian.

There are several shells available in Linux. Raspbian uses the **Bourne again shell** (**bash**) This shell is by far the most common shell used in Linux.

```
root@raspberrypi:~# apt-get install screen
Reading package lists... Done
Building dependency tree
Reading state information... Done
The following NEW packages will be installed:
  screen
0 upgraded, 1 newly installed, 0 to remove and 0 not upgraded.
Need to get 616 kB of archives.
After this operation, 1,024 kB of additional disk space will be used.
Get:1 http://ftp.uk.debian.org/debian/ squeeze/main screen armel 4.0.3-1
6 kB]
Fetched 616 kB in 0s (1,194 kB/s)
Selecting previously deselected package screen.
(Reading database ... 49685 files and directories currently installed.)
Unpacking screen (from .../screen_4.0.3-14+b1_armel.deb) ...
Processing triggers for man-db ...
Processing triggers for install-info ...
Setting up screen (4.0.3-14+b1) ...
root@raspberrypi:~# screen bash
```

Bash is an extremely powerful piece of software. One of bash's most powerful features is its ability to run scripts. A script is simply a collection of commands stored in a file that can do things, such as run a program, read keys from the keyboard, and many other things. Later on in this book, you will see how to use bash to make the most from your Raspberry Pi!

Shell utilities

A command interpreter is not much of use without any commands to run. While bash provides some very basic commands, all the other commands are shell utilities. These shell utilities together form one of the important parts of Raspbian (essential as without the utilities, the system would crash). They provide many features that range from copying files, creating directories, to the Advanced Packaging Tool (APT) – a package manager application that allows you to install and remove software from your Raspberry Pi.

You will learn more about APT later in this book.

The X.Org graphical server

After the shell and daemons are loaded, by default the X.Org graphical server is automatically started. The role of X.Org is to provide you with a common platform from which to build a graphical user interface. X.Org handles everything from moving your mouse pointer, listening, and responding to your key presses to actually drawing the applications you are running onto the screen.

The desktop environment

It is difficult to use any computer without a desktop environment. A desktop environment lets you interact with your computer using more than just your keyboard, surf the Internet, view pictures and movies, and many other things. A GUI normally uses Windows, menus, and a mouse to do this.

Raspbian includes a graphical user interface called Lightweight X11 Desktop Environment or LXDE. LXDE is used in Raspbian as it was specifically designed to run on devices such as the Raspberry Pi, which only have limited resources.

Later in this book, you will learn how to customize and use LXDE to make the most of your Raspberry Pi.

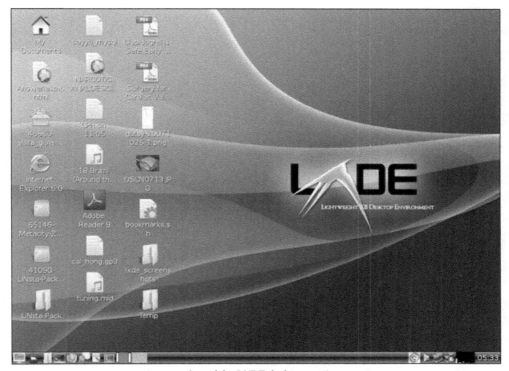

A screenshot of the LXDE desktop environment

Summary

In this chapter, you learnt what the Raspberry Pi is, about the Raspberry Pi Foundation and its history. You also learnt the basic building blocks of an operating system in general, and Raspbian in particular. In the next chapter, we will learn how to get your shiny new Raspberry Pi up and running!

2
Getting Started with Raspbian

Now that you know a bit more about Raspbian, it is time to get started. The first thing that you need to do is plug in your Raspberry Pi and then install Raspbian onto an SD card. This process is different from installing software onto your Windows PC or Mac.

In this chapter, we will cover the following topics:

- SD card specifications
- Downloading Raspbian
- Imaging Raspbian onto your SD card

SD card specifications

It is recommended that your SD card has the following specifications:

Capacity	At least 8 GB
Class	Class 4 is minimum but class 10 is recommended

 Make sure that you get the correct SD card. Raspberry Pi A and Raspberry Pi B both use a full-sized SD card. Raspberry Pi B+ uses a mini SD card.

It is highly recommended that you don't run your Raspberry Pi without an SD card. This is because all the hardware on your Raspberry Pi will not be set up correctly. This might lead to the damage of your Raspberry Pi hardware.

Downloading Raspbian

Now that you have got all the hardware, you need to get your Raspberry Pi up and running. It is time to get the Raspbian image. You can download the Raspbian image from several places. The easiest place from which you can download this is directly from the Raspberry Pi Foundation website at http://www.raspberrypi.org/downloads/.

The official Raspbian download page

On this page, you will see links to all the official operating systems supported by the Foundation. We are interested in the Raspbian image. If you are able to download the image from a BitTorrent client, you can help the Foundation save some bandwidth. If you can't do this, simply download the zip file.

At the time of writing this book, the latest version of Raspbian is based on Debian Wheezy, which was released in January 2015. The download itself is just over 800 MB. When you have downloaded the file, you need to extract the image from the zip file. How you do this depends on the operating system that you are running.

You are now ready to image Raspbian onto your SD card.

Imaging Raspbian onto your SD card

The file that you have just downloaded is an exact replica of the all the contents of an SD card. For this reason, you can't simply copy the file onto the SD card and be up and running. To copy Raspbian onto your SD card, you need to write the image directly to your SD card. The process to do this varies depending on your operating system.

Writing the image using Windows

To write the Raspbian image to an SD card using Windows, you need a software program that is capable of performing the task. There are several programs available, but we will be using a program called Win32 Disk Imager. Win32 Disk Imager is an open source tool designed to write image files to a removable storage device such as an SD card or USB drive. You can get Win32 Disk Imager from `http://sourceforge.net/projects/win32diskimager/`. Its icon will look like the following:

The steps to be performed for writing the image using Windows are as follows:

1. The first step is to insert the SD card into your computer.
2. You then need to download and install Win32 Disk Imager.
3. Once you have done this, you need to run the file that you have just downloaded and install Win32 Disk Imager.
4. You need to run Win32 Disk Imager as an administrator. To do this, right-click on the **Win32DiskImager** shortcut and click on **Run as Administrator**.
5. Once you have launched Win32 Disk Imager, you should see the following screen:

6. You now need to click on the folder button and browse to the Raspbian image that you downloaded previously. At the time of writing this book, the image file is called `2015-01-31-wheezy-raspbian.img`. The file might be compressed inside a zip file. If this is the case, you will need to extract the `.img` file first.

7. The next step is to make sure that you select the correct drive your SD card, in the **Device** drop-down list.

It is really important to double-check that you have selected the correct device, as you will be destroying all the files on the drive. You can make sure that you are selecting the correct disk by going into Windows explorer and making a note of the drive that matches the size and label of the SD card you have just inserted.

It is a good idea to remove any other removable storage devices when you do this, as this will ensure that they are not selected by mistake.

8. When you are satisfied that you have selected the correct device, click on **Write**. The write process will take a few minutes depending on the machine, and it might be a good idea to grab a cup of coffee! When this is done, you are ready to get started with your Raspberry Pi.

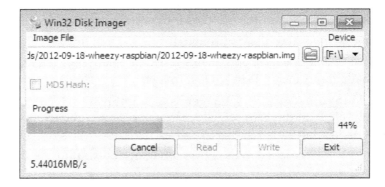

Writing the image using Mac

You are able to write the image file that you downloaded from the Raspberry Pi Foundation using Mac OS X. You don't even need to install any additional software onto your Mac to do this.

These instructions are for OS X 10.10 (Yosemite), but they will also work on previous versions of OS X.

The steps to be performed for writing the image using Mac are as follows:

1. First, you need to insert your SD card into your Mac and ensure that all other removable storage devices are unplugged so that they don't get erased by mistake.

2. Now that the SD card is inserted, we need to find out what internal device name has the operating system given to the SD card. The device name will be in the form /dev/diskX. We do this by clicking on the Apple symbol in the top-left corner and selecting **About this Mac**, as shown here:

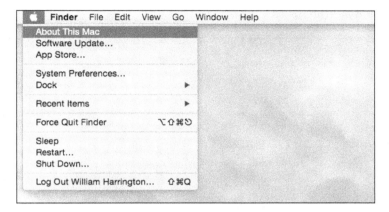

3. Now, you need to select **System Report...** as shown in the following screenshot:

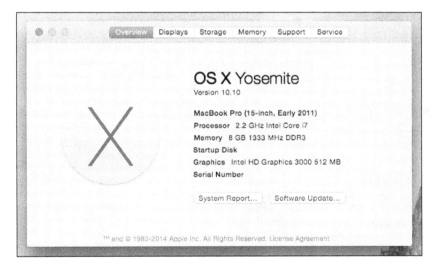

4. You will then see the system report on your screen. If your Mac has an internal SD card reader, you need to select **Card Reader** on the left-hand side of the screen.

5. If you are using a USB-to-SD card reader, you need to select **USB** and then find your SD card reader in the list.

6. After you have selected the SD card, look at the bottom of the page for **BSD Name**. It will be something similar to disk2 (in this case, **disk2s1**). This name is the internal name that the OS X kernel gives the SD card.

If there are other partitions in the card, they will be listed as diskXs1, diskXs2, and so on. We only need the diskX part.

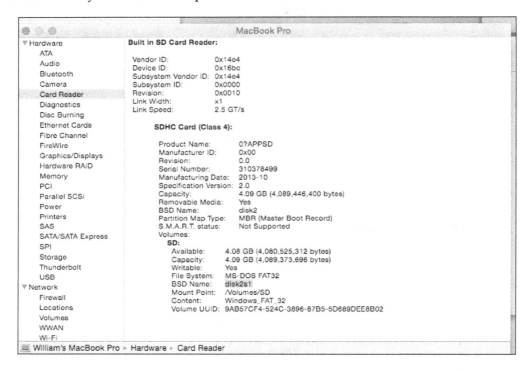

Now that we have the BSD name of the SD card, we need to make sure that none of the partitions on the SD card are mounted, but we don't want to eject the card either. By using Disk Utility, we can do this as follows:

1. First, we need to open up Disk Utility. You can find Disk Utility by navigating to **Applications | Utilities**.

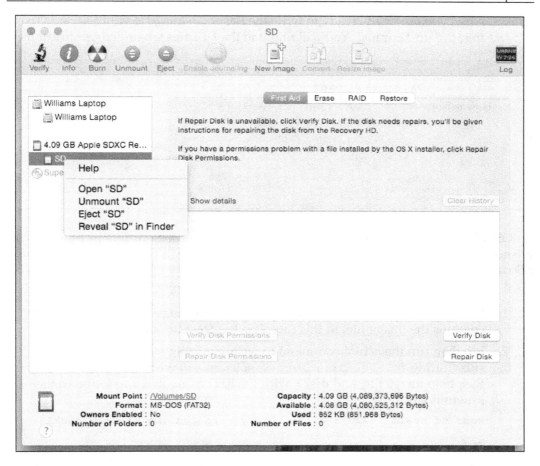

2. Once you have opened up Disk Utility, you will find your SD card on the left-hand side in the list of devices. You need to right-click on every partition in the list and select **Unmount**. This will stop the operating system from using the partition. If you don't do this, you will get a **Device in use** message when you actually write the image to the SD card.

3. Now, you are finally ready to write the Raspbian image to your SD card. To do this, fire up Terminal. You will find it in the **Utilities** tab under **Applications**.

```
●  ●  ●                                              Desktop — bash — 154×43
Last login: Wed Jul 23 14:48:53 on ttys000
Williams-MacBook-Pro:~ williams$ cd Desktop/
Williams-MacBook-Pro:Desktop williams$ sudo dd if=2014-06-20-wheezy-raspbian.img of=/dev/disk2
```

As OS X is based on the BSD operating system, we have access to all of its utilities. We are going to use a utility called **Disk Dump** (**dd**) to actually write the image file to our SD card. The dd utility is designed to read and write raw data from devices and can be used for anything from copying hard drives to writing images to SD cards.

1. Once you have opened Terminal, you need to change to the directory that contains the image file. In this case, it is the **Desktop** folder, cd Desktop.

2. We then run the actual command to write the image to the SD card, substituting 2015-01-31-wheezy-raspbian.img with the name of your Raspbian image file, and diskX with the BSD name that you found in the previous steps:

    ```
    sudo dd bs=1m if=2015-01-31-wheezy-raspbian.img of=/dev/diskX
    ```

    This command runs the dd command as a super user. The dd command reads the image file 2015-10-31-wheezy-raspbian.img and writes it to the SD card. It writes the data in chunks of one megabyte.

3. You will be asked for your administrator's password when you run this command. This command will take anywhere up to half an hour to write the image to your SD card, depending on its speed.

When this is done, insert the card into your Raspberry Pi and you are ready to go.

Writing the image using Linux

The process of writing the Raspbian image that you have just downloaded using Linux is straightforward. As mentioned, there are many different distributions of Linux. The steps that follow are tested on Ubuntu, a distribution of Linux that, like Raspbian, is based on Debian. As mentioned previously, make sure that all your removable storage devices are unplugged so that they are not accidently erased.

The first thing that we need to do is launch a terminal. A terminal is available in all the different Linux environments. In the case of Ubuntu, it is called **Terminal**. The following screenshot shows you how to find the terminal application in the latest version of Ubuntu:

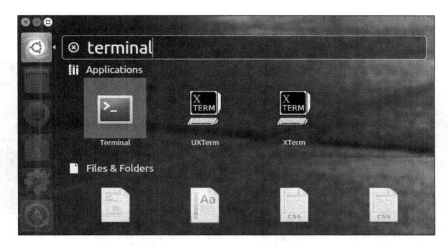

Now that you have launched the terminal, you need to gain root permissions as follows:

1. The easiest way to do this is to run the following command:

   ```
   sudo -i
   ```

2. `sudo` gives administration permissions to any program that you run in the terminal. This is necessary as writing the image to your SD card is an operation that can affect all the users. `sudo` is discussed further later in this book. You will see a terminal similar to what is shown in the following screenshot:

3. Now you are ready to find out the device name of your SD card. To do this, run the df command. The df command allows you to find out how much storage is available for each storage device that is attached to your computer. We need to run the following command:

```
df -h
```

4. The following screenshot shows the output:

```
root@ubuntu: ~
root@ubuntu:~# df -h
Filesystem      Size  Used Avail Use% Mounted on
/dev/sda1        75G   12G   60G  16% /
none            4.0K     0  4.0K   0% /sys/fs/cgroup
udev            1.9G  4.0K  1.9G   1% /dev
tmpfs           386M  1.5M  384M   1% /run
none            5.0M     0  5.0M   0% /run/lock
none            1.9G  152K  1.9G   1% /run/shm
none            100M   48K  100M   1% /run/user
/dev/sdb1       3.9G  1.3G  2.6G  33% /media/pr/80F1-0EA7
root@ubuntu:~#
```

The results obtained by running the df -h command are shown in the preceding screenshot. We can see that in this case, the SD card we are using is /dev/sdb1. If your machine has a built-in SD card reader, this can be called /dev/mmcblk0p1. Regardless of the device name, we only need the first part of the name. In the preceding example, we will use /dev/sdb, or in the case of /dev/mmcblk0p1, we will use /dev/mmcblk0. An easy way to double-check whether you have chosen the correct device is to check the size.

Now that you have got the name of your device, you need to unmount the SD card. To do this, we will use the unmount command. We do this by running the following command in your terminal for the device name that we just found:

```
umount /dev/sdb1
```

Now we are finally ready to write the image to our SD card. To do this, we need to change into the directory in which you have downloaded the Raspbian image. We then run the dd application. As mentioned in the previous section, the dd utility is designed to read and write raw data from devices and can be used for anything from copying hard drives to writing images to SD cards. The following command runs the dd command as a super user:

```
cd Desktop
dd bs=1m if=2014-06-20-wheezy-raspbian.img of=/dev/sdb1
```

The dd command reads the image file 2015-01-31-wheezy-raspbian.img and writes it to the SD card. It writes the data in chunks of one megabyte.

This command can take anywhere from a few minutes up to half an hour, depending on the size of your SD card. When this is done, insert the SD card into your Raspberry Pi and you are ready to go.

Summary

In this chapter, you learned where to download the Raspbian image from. You also stepped through how to write the Raspbian image to your SD card using several different operating systems. The next chapter will show you how to set up your Raspberry Pi and configure Raspbian.

3
Starting Raspbian

This chapter will run you through how to set up your Raspberry Pi, start Raspbian for the first time, and configure your camera if you have one.

In this chapter, we will cover the following topics:

- The different types of Raspberry Pi
- Plugging in your Raspberry Pi
- Booting your Raspberry Pi for the first time
- The Raspberry Pi Software Configuration Tool
- Finishing up
- Troubleshooting common problems

By the end of this chapter, you should have your Raspberry Pi up and running.

Raspberry Pi Model A and Raspberry Pi Model B

The Raspberry Pi A and Raspberry Pi B models are the original versions of Raspberry Pi:

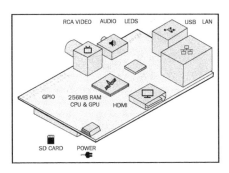

Raspberry Pi A+

Raspberry Pi A+ is the latest version of Raspberry Pi. Raspberry Pi A+ has a couple of differences from the previous version of Model A. The following are the major differences:

- Raspberry Pi A+ uses a micro SD card
- It has a larger, 40-pin I/O connector
- You now need an adaptor cable if you want to use the AV output to connect your Raspberry Pi A+ to a TV.

The Raspberry Pi A+ is shown below:

Raspberry Pi B+

The Raspberry Pi B+ is the other latest update of Raspberry Pi. Raspberry Pi B+ has a couple of differences from previous versions. These are the major differences:

- Raspberry Pi B+ uses a micro SD card
- It has a larger, 40-pin I/O connector
- You now need an adaptor cable if you want to use the AV output to connect your Raspberry Pi B+ to a TV
- Raspberry Pi B+ has a total of four USB ports instead of two

The Raspberry Pi B+ is shown below:

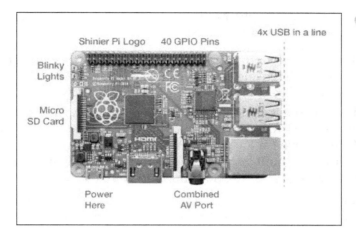

Plugging in your Raspberry Pi

It is really easy to plug in your Raspberry Pi and get it up and running. You will need a couple of things, as follows:

- Power supply
- Monitor
- Keyboard and mouse
- SD card
- Network connection

Let's go through these in detail.

Power supply

Raspberry Pi is really easy to power. It runs on a standard 5V micro USB supply. If you have a mobile phone charger with micro USB, then you should be able to use this in order to run your Raspberry Pi. You can also use a micro USB cable that is plugged into a USB phone charger.

We recommend that you use a dedicated micro USB power supply rather than a USB cable for maximum reliability. These will be available at the retailer from who you bought your Raspberry Pi.

It is important that the power supply be capable of supplying at least 1 amp. Anything less than this and you might run into intermittent resets and other problems.

Monitor

To make the most of your Raspberry Pi, you need a monitor. Raspberry Pi supports two different types of monitors:

- **HDMI**: This is a modern connector that supports the sending of both high-definition video and audio through one cable. All modern TVs and more and more computer monitors support HDMI.
- **AV**: This is an older standard that lets you connect your Raspberry Pi to an older TV. Both Raspberry Pi A and B have a standard AV connector at the side. If you have a Raspberry Pi A+ or B+ you can see that the AV connector is now built into the headphones connector, and you will need to buy an adaptor to be able to connect to your TV.

When you connect your Raspberry Pi to your monitor, it is important to make sure that you select the input on your monitor as the input you are using.

It is important to remember that you don't need a monitor to operate a Raspberry Pi once you have it up and running. It is, however, quite difficult to initially configure your Raspberry Pi without one.

Keyboard and mouse

A Raspberry Pi supports almost all USB keyboards and mouse. If you have a Raspberry Pi A or B, these will take both the USB ports that you have. Unless you have a Raspberry Pi B+ with four USB ports, we highly recommend that you plug a USB hub into your Raspberry Pi so that you have a few extra USB ports that you can use. You can check whether your keyboard and mouse are supported by going to `http://elinux.org/RPi_USB_Keyboards`.

SD card

You have already prepared an SD card in the previous chapter with Raspbian on it. You will need to plug this SD card into the Raspberry Pi. Make sure that you don't unplug the SD card while the Raspberry Pi is running.

Network connection

To be able to make the most of your Raspberry Pi, you will need a connection to the Internet. Raspberry Pi B and B+ both come with an Ethernet connector with which you can plug your Raspberry Pi into your router. To connect your Raspberry Pi to the Internet using Wi-Fi, you will need a USB to Wi-Fi adaptor. If you want to connect a Raspberry Pi A or A+ to the Internet using Wi-Fi, you will need to use a powered USB hub.

Plugging in your Raspberry Pi

Booting your Raspberry Pi for the first time

Now that you have everything ready, it is time to turn on your Raspberry Pi. The first thing that you need to do is make sure that your monitor is set to the correct input. This is important if you want to use HDMI, because if your Raspberry Pi doesn't detect an HDMI monitor during the boot process, it will automatically use the default AV out.

The bootloader

When you power on your Raspberry Pi, you will see the Raspberry Pi boot screen.

The Raspberry Pi bootloader

If you see this, it means that all the bootloader files on your SD card have been found and the appropriate monitor has successfully been detected. If you don't see this, then make sure that all the cables are plugged in, your monitor or TV is on the correct input, and you have imaged the SD card correctly.

The Linux kernel

The next step in the boot process is the initialization of the Linux kernel. The Linux kernel is contained inside the `kernel.img` file on your SD card.

Booting Raspbian

You will see a screen similar to the preceding screenshot as your Raspberry Pi boots up. The first boot process will take a bit longer than subsequent boots. As this is the first time that your Raspberry Pi has booted up, it will automatically load the **Raspberry Pi Software Configuration Tool**.

You can use this tool to configure different parts of your Raspberry Pi.

The Raspberry Pi Software Configuration Tool

The **Raspberry Pi Software Configuration Tool** is designed to be an easy and intuitive way to set up your Raspberry Pi. It is automatically launched when your Raspberry Pi is powered on for the first time.

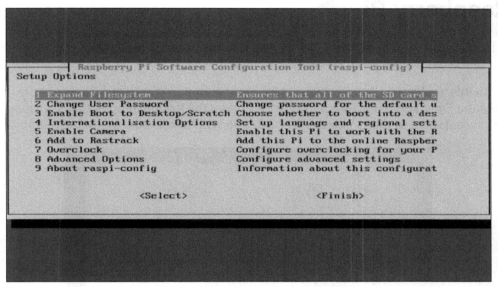

The Raspberry Pi Software Configuration Tool

The **Raspberry Pi Software Configuration Tool** is extremely easy to use. To move between menus, use the arrow keys and the **Tab** button. To select a menu, simply press the *Enter* key.

You can run the **Raspberry Pi Software Configuration Tool** whenever you want by running the following command:

```
raspi-config
```

Setting up the Raspberry Pi

Now that your Raspberry Pi has launched the **Raspberry Pi Software Configuration Tool**, it is time to use it to get your Raspberry Pi up and running.

Resizing the root filesystem of your Raspberry Pi

The first thing that you need to do is expand the filesystem of your Raspberry Pi to the full size of your SD card. If you don't do this, you won't be able to use the rest of the storage on your SD card.

To do this, make sure that the **Expand Filesystem** option is selected. Now, simply press the *Enter* key. Your root partition that stores the Raspbian operating system will now be enlarged to the size of the SD card. You will then see the following menu:

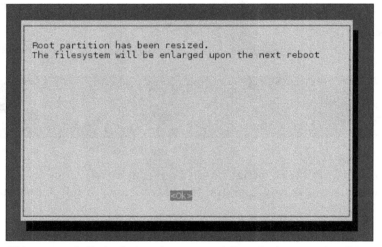

This message indicates that you have successfully resized your root partition

Changing the default password for the Raspberry Pi

The default user password for Raspbian is pi. This is not very secure and you might want to change this to something else. The **Raspberry Pi Software Configuration Tool** makes it extremely easy to do this.

1. Select the **Change User Password** option and then press *Enter*.

2. Now, you will see the first step to changing your password. When you are ready, press **<ok>**:

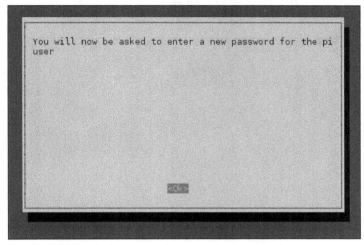

The first step to changing your password

3. You will then be prompted to enter your password. You won't see anything appearing as you type.

4. When you have finished entering your password, press *Enter*; type it again and press *Enter*. Make sure that you don't forget your password, as you will need it to install any new software onto your Raspberry Pi.

Changing the password

Enable boot to Desktop/Scratch

Raspbian has several different interfaces that you can make use of in your Raspberry Pi, such as a graphical desktop environment, Command Prompt, and the programming language called Scratch.

We recommend that you select the **Desktop Login** option so that you can make use of the graphical interface that is included in Raspbian. You can use Command Prompt and the Scratch language from the graphical interface. The default option is to use Command Prompt when your Raspberry Pi boots up.

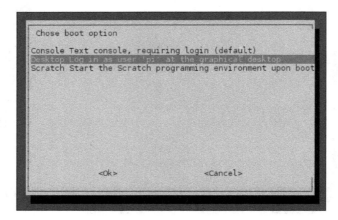

Internationalisation Options

By default, Raspbian is configured for use in the United Kingdom. For those who aren't in the United Kingdom, you need to configure Raspbian to use the correct time zone, keyboard layout, and regional settings.

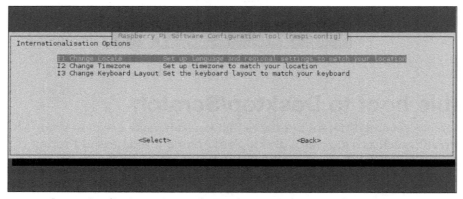

Internationalisation options in the Raspberry Pi Software Configuration Tool

Adding your locale

A locale is used to define which language Raspbian will use to display dates, numbers, currencies and so on. By default, the locale setting for your Raspberry Pi is the United Kingdom.

It is really easy to change the locale to your own country. To do this, select the **Change Locale** option.

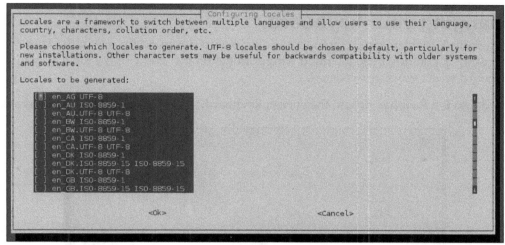

Selecting your locale

You can select multiple locales for your Raspberry Pi. In Australia, we would select the **en_AU** locale. If you were in the United States, you would select **en_US**.

Selecting your time zone

The **Raspberry Pi Software Configuration Tool** also makes it easy to select your time zone. By default, this is set to UTC. If you want the correct time to be displayed on your Raspberry Pi, you need to change your time zone.

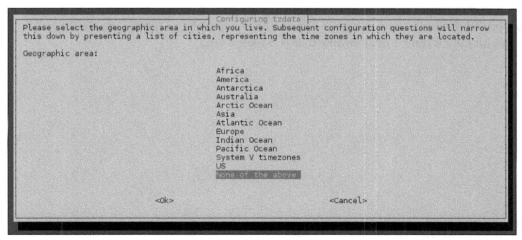

Selecting the time zone

To choose your time zone, select the region of the world you are in and press *Enter*. You can then select the city nearest to you and press *Enter*.

Changing your keyboard

By default, Raspbian expects you to use a keyboard designed for use in the United Kingdom. If you don't use a United Kingdom keyboard, many of the keys on your keyboard won't work as expected.

In order to tell Raspbian to use the correct keyboard, select **Change Keyboard Layout**.

Selecting the keyboard

If your keyboard isn't listed, go to the **Generic 101-key PC** keyboard option and press *Enter*. Depending on your location, you should be able to find a generic keyboard that will work for your country. For example, in the Unites States or Australia we would select an **English (US)** keyboard.

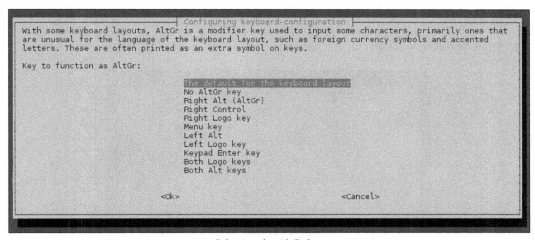

Selecting the default keyboard layout

After you've selected the keyboard, you will be asked which key you want to use as an **AltGr** key. An **AltGr** key is used in some languages to provide additional characters that aren't on the keyboard.

It is generally safe to select **The default for the keyboard layout** option.

Selecting the AltGr key

The final step to configuring your keyboard is to select which key you would like to use as the **Compose key**.

A **Compose key** lets your Raspberry Pi interpret a combination of keys as a single key press. This isn't normally needed, and it is safe to select the default option of **No compose key**.

```
                     ┤ Configuring keyboard-configuration ├
The Compose key (known also as Multi_key) causes the computer to interpret the next few keystrokes as
a combination in order to produce a character not found on the keyboard.

On the text console the Compose key does not work in Unicode mode. If not in Unicode mode, regardless
of what you choose here, you can always also use the Control+period combination as a Compose key.

Compose key:

                                 No compose key
                                 Right Alt (AltGr)
                                 Right Control
                                 Right Logo key
                                 Menu key
                                 Left Logo key
                                 Caps Lock


                <Ok>                                        <Cancel>
```

Selecting the default compose key

Enabling the Raspberry Pi camera

Raspberry Pi can be equipped with a camera. By default, it is disabled unless you have connected a camera and want to use it. To enable your Raspberry Pi camera, select the **<Enable>** option in the Raspberry Pi software configuration

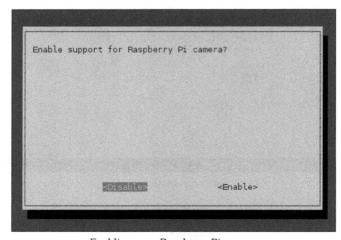

```
Enable support for Raspberry Pi camera?




                        <Disable>        <Enable>
```

Enabling your Raspberry Pi camera

Adding to Rastrack

Rastrack is a not-for-profit website that maps many of the Raspberry Pis around the world. If you want to include your Raspberry Pi on the map, select **Add to Rastrack** and enter your e-mail address.

 You can see where some of the other Raspberry Pi boards are in the world by going to http://rastrack.co.uk/.

Enabling SSH

One other useful customization that you can do in the **Raspberry Pi Software Configuration Tool** is to enable the SSH server. SSH is a secure protocol that, among other things, allows you to access Command Prompt of your Raspberry Pi remotely.

You can enable SSH by selecting **Advanced Options** in the **Raspberry Pi Software Configuration Tool**. Once there, select **A4 (SSH)** and press *Enter*. Select **Enable SSH** and you are done. This enables you to remotely access your Raspberry Pi using an SSH client, such as PuTTY and to copy files to your Raspberry Pi.

Finishing up

Now that you have customized your Raspberry Pi, it is time to start using your Raspberry Pi. To do this, you need to exit the **Raspberry Pi Software Configuration Tool** by selecting **Finish**. You will be asked to reboot your Raspberry Pi. Select **Yes** and your Raspberry Pi will reboot and load the graphical interface, which is ready to go. Remember that you can always rerun the **Raspberry Pi Software Configuration Tool** by running the following command:

```
sudo raspi-config
```

Common problems

The most common problems that people face with their Raspberry Pi come down to the power supply they are using. If your Raspberry Pi is behaving strangely, then we recommend that you try a different power supply. A good quality supply is recommended as the Raspberry Pi is susceptible to electrical noise.

It is also a good idea to check whether you have imaged your SD card correctly. It is OK to image the SD card again.

Another common problem that people have when they are setting up their Raspberry Pi for the first time is they select the wrong input on their monitor. When a Raspberry Pi boots, if it cannot find an HDMI monitor attached, it will automatically use the component output. The easiest way to stop this from happening is to make sure that the input on your monitor or TV is set to the correct input before your Raspberry Pi is turned on.

Summary

This chapter walked you through how to set up your Raspberry Pi and configure Raspbian for your region and keyboard. You also learned some of the potential problems that you might experience when you are setting up your Raspberry Pi.

In the next chapter, we will cover the Raspbian desktop environment.

4
An Introduction to the Raspbian Desktop

Now that you have got your Raspberry Pi set up and Raspbian configured, it is time to start using Raspbian on your Raspberry Pi! The Raspbian desktop is a simple, customizable, and easy-to-use desktop environment. This chapter will run you through how to customize it and some of the applications that are included with it.

We will cover the following topics in this chapter:

- The Raspbian desktop
- An introduction to the Linux filesystem
- A tour of the Raspbian desktop
- Virtual desktops
- Network management with Raspbian
- Customizing your Raspbian desktop
- Preinstalled software
- File management in Xfce

The Raspbian desktop

The Raspbian desktop is very similar to many other desktop environments, such as the Windows desktop. Raspbian is packed with heaps of educational and programming tools out of the box.

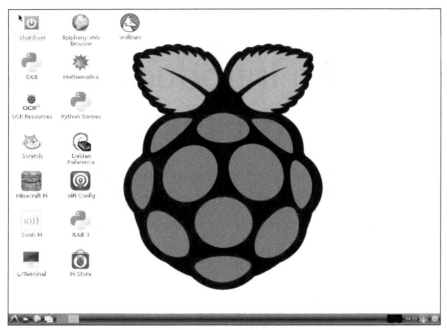

The Raspbian desktop

To be able to make the most of the desktop environment, you need to have a computer mouse connected to your Raspberry.

The Raspbian filesystem

Before we go any further, it is important to get a good understanding of how files and storage are organized on a Linux-based operating system such as Raspbian.

It won't take you long if you are used to using Windows to realize that all your files are organized differently. Gone are the drive letters that you used to access all the different storage attached to your computer. Linux, like its cousins Unix and **Berkeley Software Distribution (BSD)**, from which Mac OS X is derived, organizes everything within a filesystem hierarchy.

This filesystem hierarchy starts from one place, the root directory: /. Every file and device in Linux is contained within this single hierarchy.

An example of how this works is the /media folder. By default, if you plug a USB drive into your Raspberry Pi, Raspbian will automatically create a folder inside /media. This folder will represent the contents of your USB drive. If you have more than one storage device attached, they will all appear in /media.

A simple way to think about this is described in the Linux Documentation Project (http://www.tldp.org/):

> *"On a UNIX system, everything is a file; if something is not a file, it is a process."*

There are many different directories in a modern Linux distribution such as Raspbian that are required for it to operate. These are detailed in the following table:

Directory	Description
/	The root of the Linux filesystem.
/bin	This contains programs required to boot and use Raspbian.
/dev	All the devices attached to our Raspberry Pi are available here. The devices are represented as special files, for example sda1 and null.
/etc	This contains the configuration files for all the different software packages.
/home	Every user in the system has a folder in /home. This helps you keep each user's folders together.
/lib	Software libraries contain shared code that is shared between multiple applications. These files end in .so and are stored in this folder.
/mnt and /media	Any other filesystems that are attached to the Raspberry Pi are available inside these folders.
/opt	Software that is not installed by default with Raspbian will often be installed in this folder.
/proc	All the files inside the /proc folder are special files that allow access to various statistics and configurations in the Linux kernel.
/sbin	Any software applications that are used by system administrators to manage the system are stored inside this folder.
/tmp	Any temporary files that are used in the running of Raspbian are normally stored in /tmp. These files are normally deleted on reboot.
/usr	Any application that a normal user would install or use are installed inside this folder with their libraries and documentation.

Directory	Description
/var	/var contains all the logs and other files that are constantly changing on your Raspberry Pi.
/root	This folder is similar to the /home, but only contains files for the root user.
/boot	This folder contains the configuration files that your Raspberry Pi uses to boot.

A tour of the Raspbian desktop

There are several parts that make up the Raspbian desktop. These are the desktop, bottom panel, main menu, and panel items.

The desktop

The desktop is the main part of the screen that you see when you aren't running any programs. By default, the background image is the Raspberry Pi logo, but you will be able to change this to anything you want.

The desktop also contains all the desktop icons. The icons can be selected and dragged around the desktop. These icons start various programs when double-clicked and the icons can be moved around.

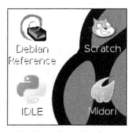

The Raspbian desktop

The bottom panel

At the bottom of the Xfce desktop, there is the taskbar. The taskbar displays all the open programs that you are running. It also contains the main menu and many panel items.

The bottom panel

On the left and right-hand sides of the bottom panel, there are several different panel items. The panel items perform various functions, such as opening a web browser or minimizing all Windows.

Some panel items

The default panel items perform the following tasks:

Icon	Task
	This opens a file manager
	This opens the default web browser
	This minimizes all the windows on the screen
	This helps you switch between virtual desktops

The main menu

In the bottom-left corner of the screen is the main menu. This menu contains many of the different programs that are preinstalled in Raspbian. These programs are split into different categories, as shown in the following screenshot The main menu is very similar to the Start menu in Microsoft Windows.

The main menu

Panel items

Panel items are small, interactive displays and buttons that show you important information without having to open a program.

By default, Raspbian includes four panel items in the bottom-right corner of the screen. These are as follows:

- CPU usage indicator
- Clock
- Screen lock button
- Power button

We can see some default panel items in the following screenshot:

Virtual desktops

Virtual desktops are really interesting additions to Xfce that aren't available by default on Windows or Mac OS X.

 Mac OS X includes Spaces (multiple desktops), however it is disabled by default. You are able to get virtual desktops in Windows using third party software such as VirtualWin.

Virtual desktops are basically like other virtual screens where you can switch back and forth between your open programs. You are able to lay out all your open programs on different virtual desktops, and then go back and forth between these virtual desktops by clicking on the virtual desktop panel item. Each of these desktops can have different backgrounds and panels. You are able to move between Windows using the *ALT + TAB* keys on the keyboard.

Two Raspbian desktops

You can create as many virtual desktops as you want using the **Openbox Configuration Manager**. These desktops can have names so you can keep track of where all your applications are.

Network management with Raspbian

To make the most of your Raspberry Pi, it needs to be connected to the Internet. You can do this in two ways: using an Ethernet cable or by Wi-Fi. Raspbian does a good job of automatically configuring its network settings for you, but sometimes you need to give it a helping hand.

Unfortunately, Raspbian doesn't include a graphical interface that lets you configure your network connections. You are able to configure your network interfaces manually using a text editor, or you can install a graphical interface to do this.

Connecting your Raspberry Pi to an Ethernet network

The Raspberry Pi Model B and Model B+ have an onboard Ethernet port. By default, Raspbian is configured to automatically get an IP address from a DHCP server on your network.

Sometimes, you might want to manually assign an IP address to your Raspberry Pi. This is done by editing a file called `interfaces`. To edit this file, you need to open up a console. The exact steps to do this are given in *Chapter 6, The Console* The command you need to run is as follows:

```
sudo nano /etc/network/interfaces
```

This will launch the nano text editor. The `interfaces` file, by default, will contain the following:

```
auto lo
iface lo inet loopback

iface eth0 inet dhcp

allow-hotplug wlan0
iface wlan0 inet manual
wpa-roam /etc/wpa_supplicant/wpa_supplicant.conf
iface default inet dhcp
```

An Ethernet port in Linux is identified by the `eth` prefix. The Ethernet port in your Raspberry Pi is called `eth0`. The `interfaces` file contains a section that configures the IP address. You will see that it is set by default to DHCP. This is where you can assign your IP address. To do this, change the `iface` line to the following lines:

```
auto eth0
iface eth0 inet static
address 192.168.2.6
netmask 255.255.255.0
gateway 192.168.2.1
```

You can see where you are able to enter your own network configuration. Once you have made the changes, press *CTRL + x* to exit nano, followed by *y* to save your changes.

To apply the changes you have made, run the following command:

```
sudo service networking restart
```

If there are any problems with your configuration, you will be notified so that you can correct them.

Connecting your Raspberry Pi to a Wi-Fi network

Raspbian supports many wireless dongles out of the box. This makes it really easy to access the Internet wirelessly from your Raspberry Pi.

You can find a list of Wi-Fi dongles that are tested and will definitely work with your Raspberry Pi at `http://elinux.org/RPi_VerifiedPeripherals`.

Connecting your Wi-Fi dongle to your Raspberry Pi

It is a good idea to plug in a Wi-Fi dongle into your Raspberry Pi; this should be done when the Raspberry Pi is off. The reason for this is that the power supply in the Raspberry Pi can sometimes have problems when USB devices are plugged in.

A Raspberry Pi B with a USB Wi-Fi dongle

Connecting to a wireless network

After you plug in your supported Wi-Fi dongle, it will be automatically detected and ready for use. Before you can go any further, you need to open the **WiFi Config** tool. The tool can be found on the Raspberry Pi desktop. After opening the tool, you will see the following window:

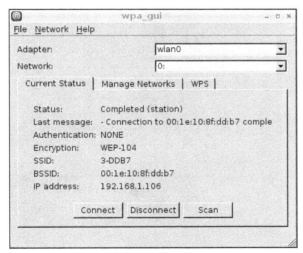

The WiFi Config tool

The **WiFi Config** tool is an easy-to-use program to connect your Raspberry Pi to your wireless network.

To connect to your wireless network, perform the following steps:

1. Click on **Scan** as shown in the following screenshot. This will list all the wireless networks within range of your Raspberry Pi. Simply double-click on your network in the list.

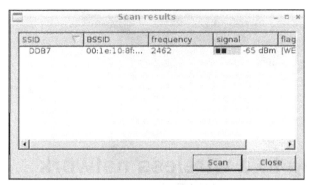

Scan results in the WiFi Config tool

2. If you have security enabled on your Wi-Fi network (it is highly recommended that you do), you will be asked to enter your wireless key.

The wireless network configuration settings

3. After entering your key, click on **Add**. You will return to the main Wireless Config Window. Simply click on your Wi-Fi network and select **Connect**.

 Did you know that WEP Wi-Fi encryption was broken in 2001, and the WEP key can now be discovered by someone with a Raspberry Pi within minutes?

Customizing your Raspbian desktop

Xfce can be customized in many different ways. This allows you to personalize the desktop environment to look the way you want it.

Changing your display resolution

The first thing that you should check when Raspbian boots to the desktop is whether the resolution your Raspberry Pi is using is suitable for your monitor. Raspbian attempts to select the correct resolution on your TV or monitor to make sure that everything looks like it should, but sometimes it is unable to do this correctly. You will be able to recognize that the resolution is wrong if the image on the screen looks blurry or doesn't fit properly.

You can change the resolution to suit your monitor using the **Monitor Settings** application in the preferences section.

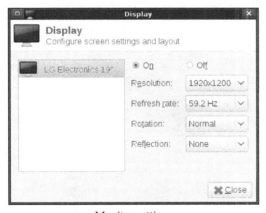

Monitor settings

It might take a few goes to find the best resolution for your monitor or TV, but it is definitely worth it! You are also able to customize the refresh rate of your monitor if you still have problems getting the display looking right.

Customizing the look and feel of your desktop

Almost every part of the Raspbian desktop can be customized, from creating extra panels to changing the default colors and fonts.

To get started, click on the main menu and inside the preferences sub menu you will see **Customise Look and Feel**. In this window, you are able to change almost everything from the default styles, colors, icons, and fonts to many other things.

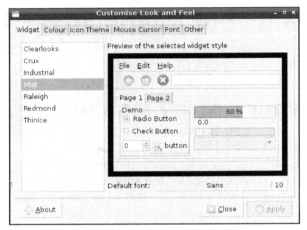

Customise look and feel dialog

One of the easiest things to customize is the style of the different UI elements. There are many different styles that you can choose from:

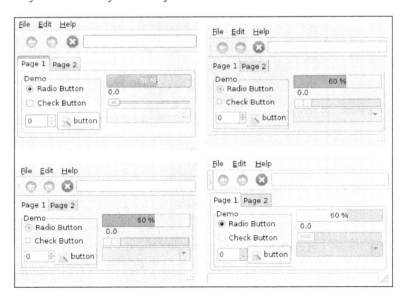

Openbox Configuration Manager

Openbox is the default Windows manager that is bundled with Raspbian. A Windows manager is responsible for the placement and appearance of Windows in a desktop environment.

You can also customize your desktop using **Openbox Configuration Manager**, which is found in **Preferences**.

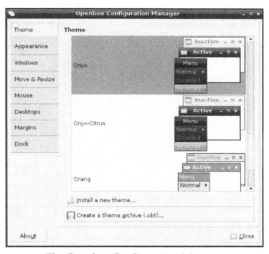

The Openbox Configuration Manager

You can install any themes designed for Openbox on your Raspberry Pi. There are many different themes preinstalled that you can choose from, or you can download many themes from the Internet. One such website that you can download themes from is `http://box-look.org/`.

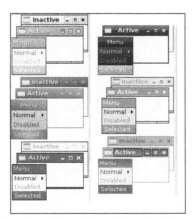

Examples of the different Openbox themes

Many other parts of the Raspberry Pi desktop can be customized using the **Openbox Configuration Manager**, ranging from how the titles of all the windows are displayed to how you resize the windows.

The best way to see all the ways in which you can customize your desktop is to have a play!

Changing the default background picture

The desktop background of your Raspberry Pi can be easily customized. To do this, simply right-click on an empty spot on your desktop to bring up a menu:

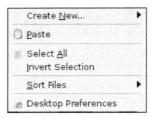

The desktop context menu

From the menu, select **Desktop Preferences**; this will bring up the **Desktop Preferences** menu.

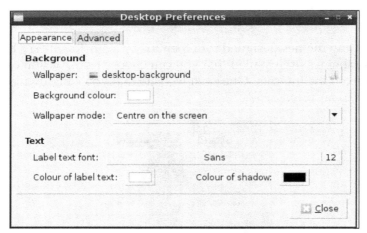

The desktop preferences dialog

The desktop preferences menu lets you customize all sorts of things on the desktop. To change the default image that you see on the background, simply click on the select box labeled **Wallpaper**, and choose the picture you want. There are several pictures included in Raspbian to get you started, and you are able to get more from other places on the Internet.

You can change the background color on the desktop, and you can also view how the background image is displayed by changing the **Wallpaper mode** and **Background color**.

Customizing your panels

Panels are a really nice feature of Xfce. Panels can be added to any part of the screen, and they can contain any number of panel items, which can be anything from a button to a graph.

A customized panel

Adding a new panel

By default, you have one panel at the bottom of the screen. You are able to add as many of these as you want in any position. Be careful before you add too many, as too many panels can slow down your Raspberry Pi!

To add a panel, right-click on an empty spot on a panel that you already have and select **Create New Panel**. The corresponding dialog will appear.

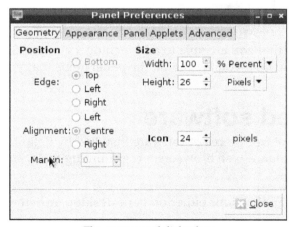

The create panel dialog box

From here, you can configure almost any aspect of your new panel, including its position, width, and appearance. You can also add panel items. When you click on **Close**, your new panel will appear, ready for you to add panel items to.

You can customize the size and shape of the existing panels by right-clicking on the panel that you want to resize and selecting **Panel settings**. This will bring up the same preceding dialog.

Adding and removing panel items

By default, there are only a few panel items on the main panel. There are almost twenty other types of panel items available by default in Xfce. It is really easy to add some of these to your panels.

To do this, right-click on the panel that you want to add the panel items to and select **Add / Remove Panel Items**.

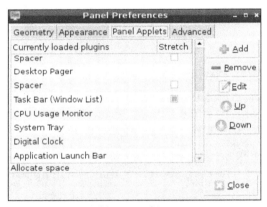

Adding panel items

Some of the widgets that you are able to add include a volume control, custom menu, and a spacer to help you lay out all the panel items that you have.

Preinstalled software

There are hundreds of free pieces of software installed by default with Raspbian. These include a calculator, web browsers, programming tools, and serious scientific applications.

You will find all the applications either on your desktop or in the main menu.

Web browsers

There are three web browsers installed by default with Raspbian. These are Epiphany, Dillo, and Netsurf. Each of these web browsers are designed for different purposes. It is also possible to install a version of Firefox onto your Raspberry Pi called Ice Weasel. This will be covered in *Chapter 6, The Console*.

Epiphany

Epiphany (now called Web) is a free, easy-to-use web browser that has a clean and minimalistic user interface. It uses the WebkitGTK+ rendering engine, similar to what is used in many other web browsers such as Safari and Google Chrome.

It is a fast, fully-fledged web browser with support for JavaScript and all modern web standards. It is highly recommended as your first choice of web browser on your Raspberry Pi.

The Epiphany web browser

Dillo

Dillo is a small, fast, minimalistic web browser designed for older, slower computers or embedded devices such as the Raspberry Pi that have a limited amount of memory and processing power.

Dillo does not support JavaScript or any other type of scripting. Because of this, it has trouble browsing most modern websites. It is, however, the fastest web browser on the Raspberry Pi and is highly recommended for browsing older websites.

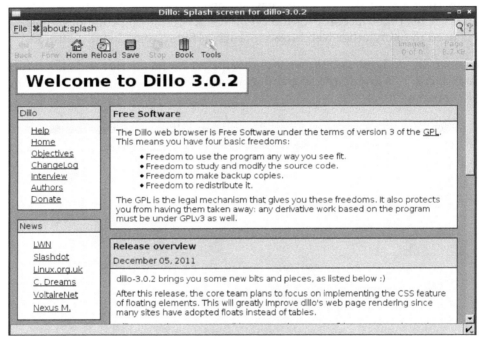

The Dillo web browser

Netsurf

Netsurf is another interesting web browser that has been included in Raspbian. Netsurf is unique, as it uses its own rendering engine called bespoke.

Netsurf was originally developed to run on RiscOS but has since been ported to many other older platforms such as AmigaOS and Haiku. Netsurf also has another interesting feature: it can be run without any other graphical support software such as X11. This makes it ideally suited for an extremely secure web kiosk.

Unfortunately, Netsurf does not support JavaScript, making it unsuitable for browsing modern websites. Plans to fix this issue are in place for version 4.

The Netsurf web browser

LXTerminal

LXTerminal is the default terminal emulator that is included with Xfce. LXTerminal allows you to run console applications inside the graphical environment of Xfce and acts as a bridge between you and your Raspberry Pi, similar to what Xfce does. We will discuss using LXTerminal in more detail in the following chapters.

Multiple instances of LXTerminal can be run, which allow you to run several terminal applications at the same time. These instances can be in their own windows or in a tab.

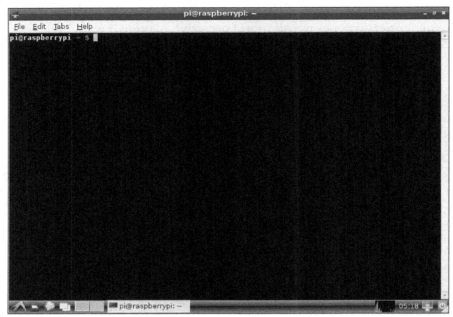

LXTerminal

Sonic Pi

Sonic Pi is one of the most exciting packages included in Raspbian. It is a free sound synthesizer that allows the user to create sound effects using a programming language. Sonic Pi has already been used to create many amazing sound effects. You can expect to hear more about it in the future!

It is designed for teachers, with extensive classroom trials to make it really easy to teach and use. You can hear Sonic Pi in action by going to http://sonic-pi.net/.

Sonic Pi in action

Debian Reference

As previously discussed, Raspbian is based on the Debian operating system. The Debian Reference application that is preinstalled on your Raspberry Pi is an excellent reference guide to almost every part of the operating system. The **Debian Reference** opens up in a web browser and is many hundreds of pages long. It is freely distributed and is well worth a read.

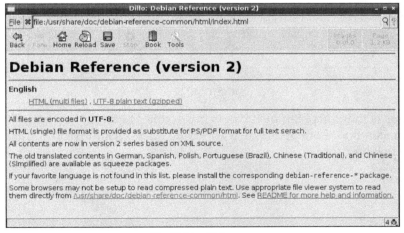

The Debian Reference

Integrated Development Environment

IDLE (Integrated Development Environment) is a simple Python development tool designed for programming in Python. Python is an easy-to-learn, highly readable, and general purpose programming language. Raspbian also includes IDLE 3, a version of IDLE that supports the newer Python 3 programming language.

IDLE incorporates an editor, a debugger, and a Python shell all in one easy-to-use application. The IDLE editor has built-in syntax highlighting, auto completion, and smart indenting. It integrates with the Python debugger to allow quick and easy debugging.

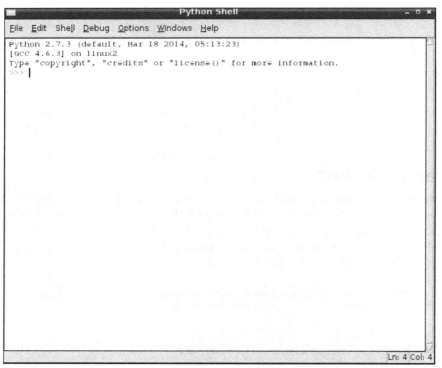

The IDLE shell

A nice bonus is that Raspbian includes many excellent games that are written in Python; you can find them at /home/pi/python_games. Simply open them up in IDLE and click on run.

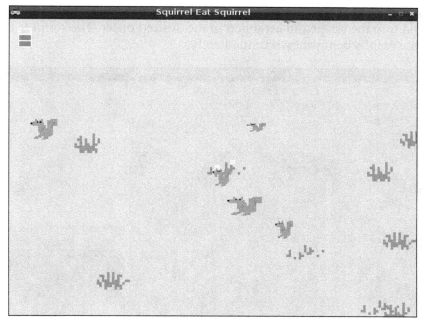

The Python game Squirrel eat Squirrel

Scratch

Continuing with the focus on education by the Raspberry Pi Foundation, Scratch is another exciting application included in Raspbian. Scratch was created by MIT Lifelong Kindergarten group in 2006.

Scratch is an easy-to-use program with a graphical programming language that allows you to create animations and games. It is an event-driven programming language that is based around sprites (a sprite is an image). The sprites can move and respond to events.

The sprites can be drawn using the built-in drawing program or imported into Scratch from any image.

Programming in Scratch is very visual. All the commands that control the sprites are dragged into the script and arranged in the desired order. The script is then run with the results being shown immediately.

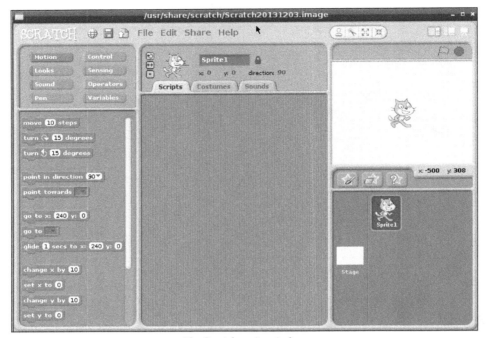

The Scratch main window

Raspbian includes many example projects as a starting point to create your first animation on your way. Over 7 million projects have been created in Scratch and uploaded to the Scratch website to be shared with other Scratch users!

You can find more information about Scratch by navigating to http://scratch. mit.edu/.

Minecraft Pi

Minecraft was created by the Swedish company Mojang in 2006 and is one of the best-selling games of all time.

Minecraft is a sandbox independent video game that was originally created by a Swedish programmer, Markus Persson. It was later published by the Swedish company Mojang. In 2014, Microsoft bought Mojang for $2.5 billion.

The aim of Minecraft is to break and move blocks. The blocks can be arranged into many different shapes. One user has even created an exact replica of the starship enterprise.

The Minecraft Raspberry Pi logo

Minecraft is available on almost every platform, including Xbox, PlayStation, iOS, Android, Raspberry Pi, and many more. It is installed by default on Raspbian.

Minecraft in Action

Pi Store

With the success of the Raspberry Pi, the Raspberry Pi Foundation wanted to have a central place for applications, games, tutorials, and tools that have been created by the Raspberry Pi. In December 2012, the Raspberry Pi Foundation created the Raspberry Pi Store.

With the Raspberry Pi Store, you have access to a huge collection of free and commercial software for your Raspberry Pi. This includes applications that are available in the store ranging from games and development tools to tutorials.

Mathematica

Mathematica is a software platform designed for scientific, engineering, and mathematical computations and includes its programming language Wolfram.. Mathematica is heavily used in education. Mathematica is a commercial product, but the Raspberry Pi Foundation worked with Wolfram Research, the company that developed Mathematica, to get it bundled with Raspbian. This is only the second time that it has been bundled; the first time was in 1988 where it was bundled with the NeXT Computer developed by Steve Jobs.

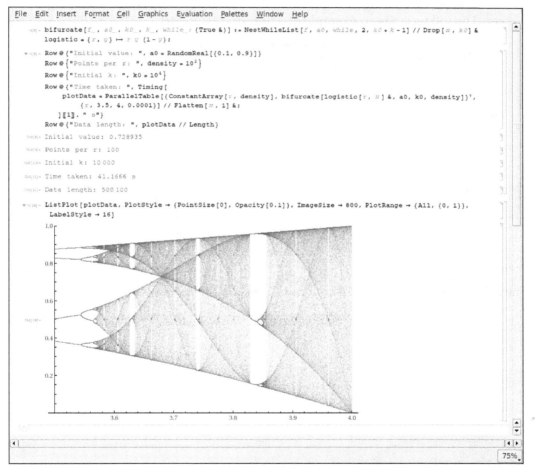

Mathematica

Mathematica includes many different features, including implementation of many different algorithms, different data visualizations, and numerical operations. It is used by almost all Fortune 500 companies and major universities. It has been an important tool used in scientific, technical, and business advancement. It has been a critical tool used by many noble prize winning scientists.

Other software included with Raspbian

There are many other pieces of software included with Raspbian that we haven't discussed here. These range from a calculator to a simple text editor and image viewer. The following is an example of a built-in calculator:

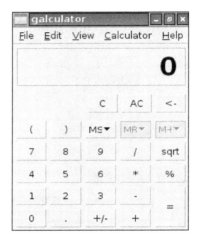

The following is an example of Leafpad – one of Raspbian's text editors:

File management in Xfce

Xfce comes with a built-in file manager. You are able to use it to browse all the storage devices attached to your Raspberry Pi. You are also able to perform various different file management action, such as copying and moving files.

You can launch the file manager using either the file manager panel item or find it in the main menu.

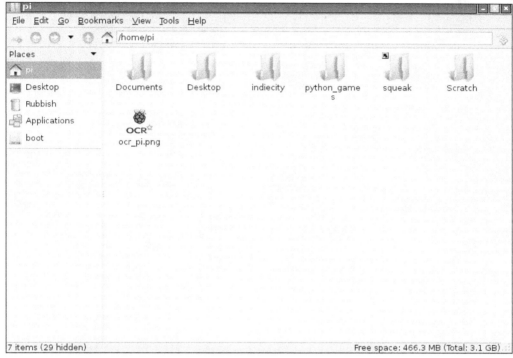

The Xfce file manager

Any additional storage that you attach to your device will appear in the **Places** menu to the left for easy access. You can also use the file manager to let you access files stored on another server. This is done using the **Network Drives** menu in the **Go** section.

The desktop of your Raspberry Pi is just another folder on your Raspberry Pi. As such, you are able to customize the icons on it by deleting or removing them. You can also create new folders and files that are stored on the desktop for easy locating.

Summary

The Raspbian desktop is a simple, easy-to-use desktop environment. It is quite different from the typical Windows and Mac OS X desktop environments, but as you have discovered it is really powerful and easy to use.

The best way to learn about the Raspbian desktop is to start exploring. Remember that if you break something, all you have to do is re-image your card and you are ready to go again!

5
Installing Software on Raspbian

The primary purpose of an operating system is to provide a consistent software platform, regardless of the underlying hardware. Once the operating system is installed, it can be expanded with many other software packages.

Raspbian is a good example of a Linux-based operating system. As Raspbian is based on Debian, it has access to its huge software repository. Raspbian initially had access to over 35,000 different software packages in the Debian repositories, but this number keeps growing.

Debian Wheezy, on which Raspbian is based, doesn't officially support the older ARMV6 CPU in the Raspberry Pi. During initial development of Raspbian in 2012, the developers spent a huge amount of time recompiling the vast collection of software in the Debian repositories for the ARMv6K architecture to get maximum performance out of the Raspberry Pi.

This chapter runs through several different methods of installing software on your Raspberry Pi.

Package management in Linux

There are many different tools available to manage software on a Linux distribution. Some of these include the APT and RPM package managers.

Raspbian uses the Advanced Packaging Tool, also known as the APT. The APT handles the dependencies of any package. Installation and removal of software packages are handled by an application called dpkg. It is the recommended way to install any software on your Raspberry Pi. Every part of Raspbian is bundled into a package.

The APT can automatically download the software that you want to install from repositories that are preconfigured. A repository is a collection of precompiled software that can be installed. These repositories are automatically selected, based on your location, to maximize download speed. It also automatically handles updates of all the software packages that are installed on your Raspberry Pi. The APT was first released in 1998 and is often hailed as one of Debian's best features.

Methods of installing software

There are several different ways to install software on your Raspberry Pi. These include:

- apt-get
- GUI Package Manager
- Aptitude
- Raspberry Pi Store
- The source

All of these methods, with the exception of installing from source code, use APT and dpkg to install the software package.

dpkg

dpkg is a software application at the center of Raspbian's software package management system. It is a software tool that actually installs a software package from a `.deb` file.

A `.deb` file contains three different parts:

- A Debian-binary file that contains the version of dpkg needed to install the package
- A control archive that has all the information needed to install the package
- A data archive that contains the actual software itself

dpkg reads the `.deb` file and determines whether all of the required software is installed. If the required software isn't installed, it will let you know what the required software is.

APT

The APT is a frontend tool that makes using dpkg a lot easier. It is preconfigured with several repositories that contain every official package that is available to be installed on your Raspberry Pi.

These repositories are split into several different archives or groups, depending on what software packages are contained in each. It is also extremely easy to add other third-party repositories.

The main archive

The main archive contains all of the software that makes up the Raspbian distribution. If the package is not in the archive, it is not considered a part of the Raspbian distribution. No packages in this archive require any software that is outside it. The Debian project requires that all packages in this archive should be free and can be distributed, modified, and shared freely. The software in this archive is supported by the Debian project.

The contrib archive

Any package that requires other packages that aren't part of the main archive is included in the contrib archive. The contrib archive may also contain wrapper packages and other pieces of free software that work with non-free software.

The non-free archive

Any other software that does not comply with the Debian project's guidelines for free software is included in the non-free archive. Other pieces of software that have problems that may affect their free distribution are included in the archive as well.

Package verification

The official Raspbian repositories are signed with a digital signature to ensure that the package does not get corrupted when it is downloaded. This is achieved using public key encryption and a digital certificate to prove that the packages in the repository are from who they say they are.

Using the console

The most common way to install software on your Raspberry Pi is by using apt-get. It is a very powerful command-line application.

To run `apt-get`, you need to use the command shell. The command shell is available for you through an application that is installed in Raspbian by default. The application is called LXTerminal.

You can launch LXTerminal by double-clicking on its icon on the desktop.

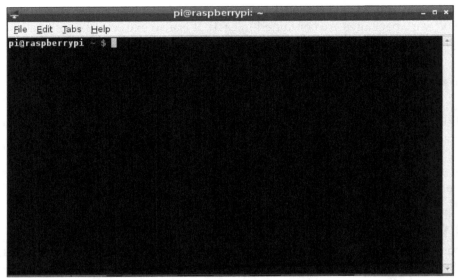

LXTerminal

LXTerminal allows you to run commands using the bash command shell (and other command shells if desired). You will learn more about the bash shell in *Chapter 6, The Console*.

Generally, each command you run fits in one line. When you have finished typing a command, simply press *Enter* to run it. The output of the program will be displayed in the following lines. If you want to rerun or modify a command that you have just typed, simply press the up arrow key on your keyboard and you will see the previous command displayed again. You will then be able to edit and rerun it by pressing *Enter* again.

Don't forget that Linux is case sensitive, so the Apt-get command won't work but apt-get will!

Linux is an inherently secure operating system. Most of the commands in this chapter require administrator permissions. It is really easy to see whether you need root permissions. If they are required, you will see the following:

```
E: Could not open lock file /var/lib/dpkg/lock - open (13: Permission denied)
E: Unable to lock the administration directory (/var/lib/dpkg/), are you root?
```

To run a command as the system administrator, simply add it to the beginning of any command that you need to run:

```
sudo
```

Depending on whether you have set a password or not, you may be asked to enter your password. Running apt-get is really simple just type apt-get and press *Enter*:

```
apt-get
```

The apt-get command will respond with a heap of information about the different options that are available. The options that we are interested in are:

* apt-get update
* apt-get install
* apt-get remove

apt-get update

The first thing that we want to do is ensure that Raspbian knows what the latest versions of software are. The apt-get update command automatically connects to the Raspbian repository and downloads the latest list of packages.

It is recommended that before installing any software, you run the apt-get update command if you haven't done so recently.

apt-get install

The real power of the apt packaging system becomes apparent when you run the install command. To actually install the software package on your Raspberry Pi, you need to run apt-get install followed by the name of the software package.

Consider the following command:

```
sudo apt-get install apache2
```

This command will install the Apache2 web server. This is one of the most popular web servers in the world, with a 59% market share at the time of writing this book. Apache2 is extremely powerful but can be quite resource heavy depending on its configuration.

You will see something similar in your console to what is shown in the following screenshot:

```
pi@raspberrypi ~ $ sudo apt-get install apache2
Reading package lists... Done
Building dependency tree
Reading state information... Done
The following extra packages will be installed:
    apache2-mpm-worker apache2-utils apache2.2-bin apache2.2-common libapr1 libaprutil1
    libaprutil1-dbd-sqlite3 libaprutil1-ldap ssl-cert
Suggested packages:
    apache2-doc apache2-suexec apache2-suexec-custom openssl-blacklist
The following NEW packages will be installed:
    apache2 apache2-mpm-worker apache2-utils apache2.2-bin apache2.2-common libapr1 libaprutil1
    libaprutil1-dbd-sqlite3 libaprutil1-ldap ssl-cert
0 upgraded, 10 newly installed, 0 to remove and 34 not upgraded.
Need to get 1,355 kB of archives.
After this operation, 4,929 kB of additional disk space will be used.
Do you want to continue [Y/n]?
```

Installing Apache2 using apt-get install

The apt-get command will automatically connect to the Internet and download the Apache2 package and all the packages that Apache2 needs to operate. You may be asked to confirm that you want to continue installing the software. Simply press the *Y* key and then *Enter*. After the package is installed and configured, your new software is ready to go!

There are many packages that are available to extend the function of Apache2. These packages won't be installed by default. If you need to install these extras, they will need to be installed manually.

There are some packages that you are able to install, called metapackages. These packages represent a collection of packages that add a particular function to your Raspberry Pi. An example of this is as follows: if you used a distribution based on Raspbian that didn't include a graphical user interface, you could install this interface in one go by installing a metapackage. These packages behave as normal packages but are actually collections of several different packages behind the scenes. You are also able to use the * wildcard to represent multiple characters. To install all the available php packages, you could run this:

```
sudo apt-get install php-*
```

apt-get remove

Sometimes, you will want to remove some software packages that have been installed and are no longer required. Removing a package is as easy as installing it. You simply use the apt-get remove command.

Run the following command:

```
sudo apt-get remove apache2
```

You should get an output similar to this:

```
pi@raspberrypi ~ $ sudo apt-get remove apache2

Reading package lists... Done
Building dependency tree
Reading state information... Done
The following packages were automatically installed and are no longer required:
  apache2-mpm-worker apache2-utils apache2.2-bin apache2.2-common libapr1 libaprutil1
  libaprutil1-dbd-sqlite3 libaprutil1-ldap ssl-cert
Use 'apt-get autoremove' to remove them.
The following packages will be REMOVED:
  apache2
0 upgraded, 0 newly installed, 1 to remove and 34 not upgraded.
After this operation, 29.7 kB disk space will be freed.
(Reading database ... 73893 files and directories currently installed.)
Removing apache2 ...
```

Removing Apache2 using apt-get remove

For a bit of fun, try running apt-get moo!

Searching for packages

There are so many packages available to install using apt-get that it can be difficult to find the package that you want to install. Fortunately, it is really easy to search for the packages that are available to be installed. To do this, you use the apt-cache search tool.

Following on from our example of using the Apache2 package, you are able to see other extensions to the Apache2 package by running this command:

```
sudo apt-cache search apache2
```

The apt-cache search tool will list all the packages that mention Apache2 in their description or require Apache2.

Synaptic GUI Package Manager

There are many different ways in which you can install software on your Raspberry Pi. Using apt-get is one way. Another way is by using a GUI tool such as the **Synaptic Package Manager.** Unfortunately, it isn't installed in Raspbian by default, but it is easily installed using apt-get.

To install synaptic, run the following command in LXTerminal:

```
sudo apt-get install synaptic
```

Synaptic will take a few minutes to install on your Raspberry Pi as it is a reasonably large application. You will find the **Synaptic Package Manager** in the **Other** submenu in the main menu.

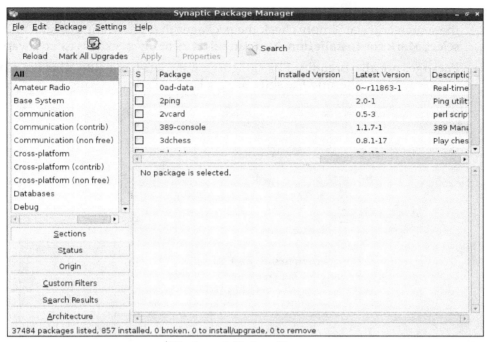

The Synaptic Package Manager

Searching and installing packages in Synaptic

You can search for packages in Synaptic using the search button:

1. Simply click on the **Search** button and enter the package that you are looking for.

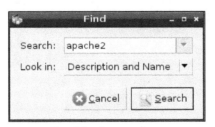

Searching for a package

2. After clicking on **Search**, you will be shown all the packages that meet the search criteria. Simply check the packages that you want to install and select **Mark for Installation**. You can select as many packages as you want.

Packages are also organized by category on the left-hand side. This is a really easy way to try and find the software packages you are looking for.

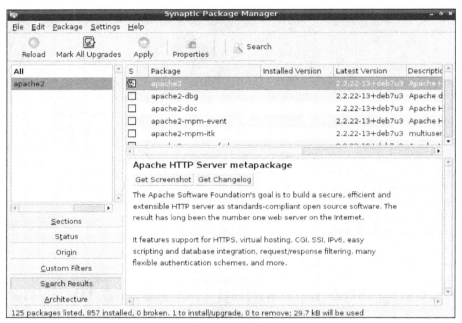

Selecting a package

3. When you click on **Apply**, Synaptic will ask you to confirm that you want to install the packages that you have selected. After you click on **Apply**, the packages will be installed.

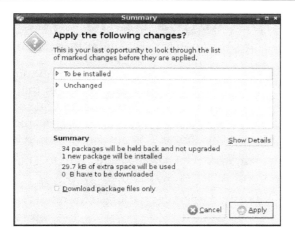

4. The package installation may take several minutes, depending on what packages you are installing. The progress of the installation can be tracked by selecting **Details**.

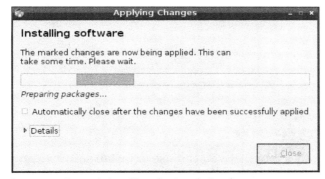

Synaptic installing the Apache2 web server

Uninstalling packages using Synaptic

Uninstalling packages using Synaptic is very similar to installing packages:

1. If you are trying to uninstall a package that you previously installed, you need to search for it. You can also see any packages that are installed by selecting the **Status** filter on the left. This will let you see all the packages that have been installed in a list. Over 850 packages are installed in the default Raspbian distribution, so it is quicker to search for them.

2. Once you have found the package that you want to uninstall, simply click on the checkbox and select `Mark for Removal`.

3. When you have finished selecting packages for removal, click on **Apply**.

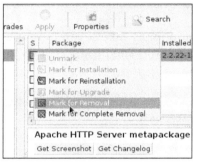

Removing a package using Synaptic

The Pi Store

The Pi Store is another tool that you can use to install software on your Raspberry Pi. The Raspberry Pi Store is installed by default in Raspbian and can be opened using the **Pi Store** icon on the desktop. **The Pi Store** groups together most of the best pieces of software that are available to be installed on your Raspberry Pi in one place.

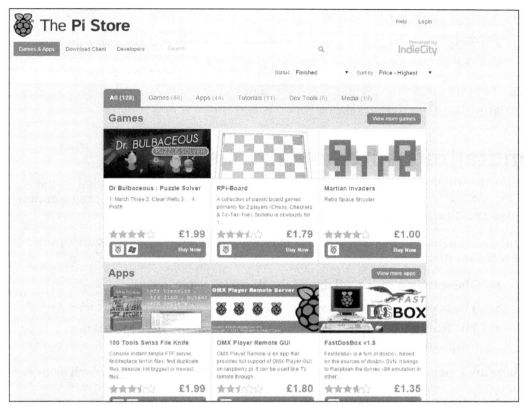

The Pi Store

The Pi Store is the only piece of software installed on your Raspberry Pi that actually sells commercial software and other content. To be able to purchase non-free software from the Pi Store, you need to register and provide a payment method such as a credit card.

The Pi Store is really easy to use:

1. Simply find the software that you want to install, and click on **Buy Now**.

2. Log in with your account, and away you go!

The Pi Store automatically handles all updates to any software that you have purchased.

Installing software from source

All software programs are built from different files. These files are called source code and are written in programming languages. The most common programming languages that are used on Linux are C and C++.

There are all sorts of reasons that you may want to download and install a piece of software that is distributed as source code. Some of these are as follows:

- The software isn't available in the Raspbian repositories.
- The latest version of the software isn't in the Raspbian repositories.
- The features in the software aren't available in the packages in the Raspbian repositories.

There are a several disadvantages to installing software from source, such as these:

- Updates aren't automatically installed for any software packages that are installed from source.
- Additional software is required to compile and install the software. Generally this is the `build-essential` metapackage.
- It can take a long time to compile and install software depending on its complexity.

If you find a software package that you want to download and install on your Raspberry Pi, the first thing you need to do is make sure that you have all the required tools to build the application:

1. The most common tools can be installed after you have installed the `build-essential` package:

   ```
   sudo apt-get install build-essential
   ```

   This will install all the software tools you need to use to compile most C and C++ applications, including the make application and the gcc and g++ compilers.

2. Now you need to download the application that you want to install. In this example, we will use the Apache2 web server. You can download Apache2 from `http://apache.mirror.serversaustralia.com.au//httpd/httpd-2.4.10.tar.bz2`.

3. You can download the source code using a web browser. Another easy way to download the code is to use the wget application. It automatically downloads a file and stores it in your Raspberry Pi:

   ```
   wget http://apache.mirror.serversaustralia.com.au//httpd/
   httpd-2.4.10.tar.bz2
   ```

   Once you source code has been downloaded on your Raspberry Pi, you need to extract the software from the archive. An archive is just a file that contains many other files that have been shrunk to make them easier to distribute.

4. To extract a `.tar.bz2` archive such as the Apache2 application, run the following command:

   ```
   tarxvfhttpd-2.4.10.tar.gz
   ```

   The exact command will vary depending on the software that you are trying to install, but will generally be very similar to the command you just used.

These commands will unpack all the files in the `Apache2` archive and put them into a folder that contains the entire `Apache2` source.

Almost all software packages that you download contain a file inside them, called `README.md`. This file generally contains instructions that you need to follow to install and build the software.

Here is the normal process you need to follow to build a software package:

- `./configure`
- `make`
- `make install`

These commands perform lot of processes. Let's start with `./configure`. The `./configure` command is a script that generates the `MakeFile` file used by `make` to compile the software. This `MakeFile` file is customized to suit your Raspberry Pi. It will also let you know whether there are any other dependencies that you need to install to be able to build the software.

The make command is the command that actually compiles the software from the source code into an application that you can run on your Raspberry Pi. This compilation process will show lots of information as it progresses, and the process may take quite a long time. The Linux kernel can take well over half an hour to compile,so it is probably best to go and grab a cup of coffee!

After the applications have been compiled, you need to install them. Fortunately, most applications include an installation script that does this for you. Simply run make install!

 Just remember that these instructions are generic and that some software packages may need to be installed differently.

Installing updates

Raspbian is constantly under development, and updates that have fixes, new features, and security improvements are continually being released. It is highly recommended that you install all the updates that are available. There are many ways to do this, including using apt get and Synaptic.

Installing updates using apt-get

The apt-get command can be used to update the software in your Raspberry Pi. The first thing you need to do is ask apt-get to get the list of all pieces of software that are available for installation on your Raspberry Pi:

```
sudo apt-get update
```

This command may take a few minutes depending on your internet connection. To perform upgrades of the packages, you need to run the following command:

```
sudo apt-get upgrade
```

This command will download and install all the latest packages from the Raspbian repositories on your Raspberry Pi. You will then be fully up to date!

Installing updates using Synaptic

Updates can also be installed using the **Synaptic Package Manager**:

1. This can be done by selecting the **Refresh** button.

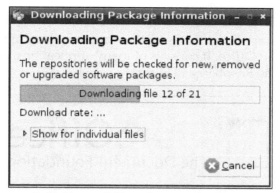

Refreshing available packages using Synaptic

2. Once the package list has been refreshed, click on **Mark All Upgrades**.

3. You will be asked to confirm the packages you are upgrading. Simply select **Mark** and then click on **Apply**, then all of the software on your Raspberry Pi will be up to date.

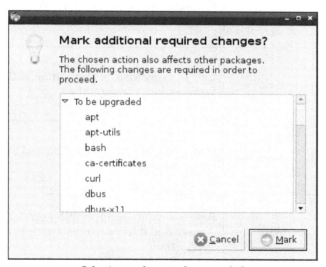

Selecting packages to be upgraded

Other software that you can install

There is only this much software that can be installed on the default Raspbian installation. Most pieces of software included in Raspbian are aimed at the educational market. Because of this, there isn't much productivity software preinstalled on your Raspberry Pi. Fortunately, this is easy to fix!

LibreOffice

LibreOffice is a free, complete office suite that contains many of the features that are also found in Microsoft Office. It consists of many applications, and is available for installation through the Raspberry Pi Store.

A few of these applications are as follows:

Icon	Name	Description
	Writer	Writer is a complete word processor with features similar to Microsoft word.
	Calc	Calc is a spreadsheet application with many features, including graphs.
	Impress	Impress is an application designed to create presentations.
	Base	Base is a database application similar to Microsoft Access, and it lets you create simple database applications

There are many other applications included in LibreOffice that aren't mentioned here. The best way to see all the features is to download LibreOffice and give it a go! You can find more information at `www.libreoffice.org`.

IceDove e-mail client

Another important productivity tool for the Raspberry Pi is the IceDove e-mail client. IceDove is the popular Thunderbird e-mail client that has been rebranded by Debian due to copyright issues with the Thunderbird and Firefox logos.

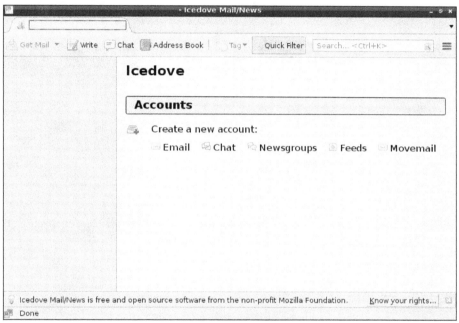

IceDove

IceDove is an excellent e-mail client and is highly recommended. You can install IceDove by running this command:

```
sudo apt-get install icedove
```

IceWeasel

Another excellent application is the IceWeasel web browser.

IceWeasel

IceWeasel is a rebranded version of Firefox, and it supports all the features that you have come to expect from a modern web browser.

You can install IceWeasel by running the following command:

```
sudo apt-get install iceweasel
```

Summary

In this chapter, you learned several ways to install software packages on your Raspberry Pi, and some of the tools that you can use to do this. Thanks to the huge Debian repositories and the open source nature of Linux-based operating systems such as Raspbian, there is so much variety in software available for the Raspberry Pi. Now that you know how to install software on this device, you simply need to start looking for what you are after.

6
The Console

Behind the pretty graphical interfaces of a Linux-based operating system such as Raspbian, is the console.

The console is the most basic way of communicating with the innards of the Raspbian operating system. The console's history started at the very beginning of computing where the interface to a computer was a keyboard and a teletype machine. At that time, operators would type a command and the result would be printed in front of them.

A teletype machine

Fortunately, with the development of computer monitors, we no longer need a typewriter to communicate with our computer and there are many different ways in which this can be done. You already learned how to use the Raspberry Pi's graphical user interface Xfce, and this chapter will run you through how you can use the built-in console terminal application called bash.

Bash

The **Bourne again shell (bash)** is a console shell developed by the GNU project that was released in 1989. Originally written by Brian Fox, it has become the de facto standard and is used by default in almost all Linux operating systems, OS X, Novell NetWare, Android, as well as on Windows. The bash was inspired by the sh shell, which was extremely popular around the time bash was created.

The bash shell was written as an open source replacement to the Bourne shell that was the default command-line interpreter for Unix. The bash supports many features, including the autocompletion of commands and filename wildcards.

Launching the bash command interpreter

The bash command interpreter is made available to us in the Xfce environment through the LXTerminal application. Other terminal clients such as Yakuake can be installed using apt-get. If you have configured Raspbian to not start the Xfce desktop environment, bash will be automatically started after you log in.

You can launch LXTerminal by double-clicking on its icon on the desktop.

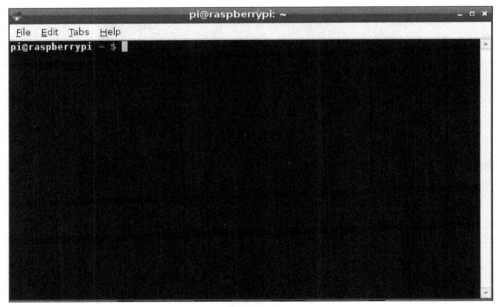

LXTerminal

You can launch and run as many instances of LXTerminal as you like, but don't forget that your Raspberry Pi doesn't have unlimited resources.

 If you are not using the Xfce desktop environment, bash will be launched when you log in.

The first thing that you will notice is that you have Command Prompt. By default, this Command Prompt will show you the current directory that you are working in, your Raspberry Pi's hostname (by default `raspberrypi`), and your username (by default this is `pi`).

As you move around the filesystem, you will see the name of the directory that you are in.

To run a command using the bash command interpreter, simply type the command and press the *Enter* key. The command will run and the results will be displayed. While a command is running, you won't be able to run other commands until it is finished.

 If you wish to let a command run in the background, all you need to do is add an & operator to the end of the command. This will let the command run in the background.

Linux is a full multiprocessing system and you can run as many instances of LXTerminal as you want. To see which processing commands are running in the background on your Raspberry Pi, simply run `ps -a`.

Basic bash commands

The best way to start learning bash is to start using it. Remember that if you really make a mess of things, all you need to do is reimage your SD card and away you go!

It is easy to get more information about any of the commands that are referred to in this chapter. You can do this using the `man` command.

The `man` command launches the built-in documentation system for Linux. Almost every command available has documentation in the man system.

For example, to find out more information about the `ls` command, simply run the following command:

```
man ls
```

This will launch the man program and display every bit of information that you need to know about the ls program.

```
LS(1)                           User Commands                           LS(1)

NAME
       ls - list directory contents

SYNOPSIS
       ls [OPTION]... [FILE]...

DESCRIPTION
       List  information  about  the  FILEs  (the current directory by default).  Sort entries
       alphabetically if none of -cftuvSUX nor --sort is specified.

       Mandatory arguments to long options are mandatory for short options too.

       -a, --all
              do not ignore entries starting with .

       -A, --almost-all
              do not list implied . and ..

       --author
              with -l, print the author of each file

       -b, --escape
              print C-style escapes for nongraphic characters

       --block-size=SIZE
              scale sizes by SIZE before printing them.  E.g., `--block-size=M' prints  sizes
              in units of 1,048,576 bytes.  See SIZE format below.

       -B, --ignore-backups
              do not list implied entries ending with ~

       -c     with  -lt:  sort  by,  and show, ctime (time of last modification of file status
 Manual page ls(1) line 1 (press h for help or q to quit)
```

The man ls command

To move around the man program, you can use the arrow keys on your keyboard. If you wish to skip the whole page, you can press the spacebar key. When you have finished reading the information, you can exit by pressing the *q* key.

 Don't forget that Linux is a case-sensitive operating system and it is extremely important that you use the correct case when you are running the command.

The autocompletion of commands

One of the most useful features of bash is its ability to autocomplete the name of the command that you are typing. This is as easy as pressing the *Tab* key.

For example, if you want to run the command `nano` in order to launch the nano text editor, simply type the following command:

`nan`

Now press the *Tab* key. The bash will automatically autocomplete the command and display this:

`nano`

This can be a real timesaver. If there is more than one possible combination of autocompletion, you will need to press the *Tab* key twice. This will cause bash to list all the different possibilities.

```
pi@raspberrypi ~ $ na
namei          nameif          nano          native2ascii  nawk
pi@raspberrypi ~ $ na
```

The bash's autocomplete system

Running commands as root

Linux is an inherently secure operating system. Every part of the operating system has been configured to be secure by default. Every file is owned by a particular user, and that user is able to allocate permissions to that file in order to restrict other users and groups from accessing the file.

By default, all commands that are run in bash are run as the current user. The current user is normally the Pi user. This user is a standard user, and this means that you will not be able to run any commands that can affect other users, such as installing software or changing the network configuration of your Raspberry Pi.

Fortunately, it is easy to run commands as the root or superuser. This user has unlimited access to every part of the operating system and must be used with caution.

To run a command as the superuser, you can use use the `sudo` utility. The `sudo` utility lets you run a command as a different user from what you are logged in as.

In order to use the `sudo` utility to run a command as root, all you need to do is prepend the command that you want to run with `sudo`.

Take an example of the following command:

`sudo apt-get moo`

It will run the `apt-get` application as root. This particular command will invoke `apt-get Easter egg`, proving that computer programmers sometimes do have a sense of humor!

```
pi@raspberrypi ~ $ sudo apt-get moo
         (__)
         (oo)
   /------\/
  / |    ||
 *  /\---/\
    ~~   ~~
....."Have you mooed today?"...
pi@raspberrypi ~ $ 
```

Running a command as root that can make your Raspberry Pi moo!

Moving around the filesystem using bash

The most basic part of using a command interpreter, such as bash, is to be able to move around the Linux filesystem. It is important to understand how bash lets you represent directories. This is done in two different ways: using **absolute paths** and **relative paths**.

Absolute paths

An absolute path is a path that describes the location of a file or folder starting from / (root). This is easy to spot as it will always start with /.

An example of an absolute path is `/home/pi/Desktop`. This path is the folder that contains all the items on your desktop.

Relative paths

A relative path is a path to the file or folder that is described based on where you are in the filesystem.

An example of a relative path is `../Desktop`. This means that a folder called `Desktop` is stored in a folder that is one level above the one you are in.

There are several special paths that you should know of in bash, as follows:

Path	Description
/	This is the root of the Linux filesystem and the highest path that you can have.
./	This represents the directory that you are currently in.
../	This is the directory one level below the one you are in.
~	This represents your home directory. When you are logged in as the Pi user, this will be /home/pi. If you are running a command as the root, this will be /root.

 If you don't have a keyboard with the ~ key, you can press *F12* instead.

Manipulating files

Now that you have an understanding of how paths are represented in bash, it is time to learn how to manipulate them.

There are many commands that you can use to manipulate files in bash, which include the commands in the following table:

ls	cd	pwd	cat	head and tail
cp	mv	rm	mkdir	touch
adduser	addgroup	passwd	chmod	chown

ls

ls is perhaps the most common basic function, and is used regularly to see which files are present in the directory that you are in. This is done using the list (ls) command. By default, this is the current folder that you are in. If you want to see the contents of another folder, simply append the path to the end of the ls command.

```
pi@raspberrypi ~ $ ls
Desktop Documents  indiecity  ocr_pi.png  python_games  Scratch
pi@raspberrypi ~ $ 
```

The contents of the home directory

ls doesn't display any files or folders that begin with (.). The reason for this is that any file or directories beginning with (.) are hidden.

The ls command has many different options that change the output on your screen. Some common ls parameters are as follows:

Option	Description
-a	This shows hidden files and folders
-l	This uses the long list format. This will show file sizes, file permissions, and the owners of the files
-h	This shows all the files sized in a human-readable format

cd

The Linux filesystem is made up of many different files and folders. When using bash, it is really important to be able to move around the filesystem. This is done using the cd (change directory) command.

cd is easy to use. All you need to do in order to change the current directory is to run cd followed by the path of the folder you want to move into. This can either be an absolute directory or a relative directory.

```
pi@raspberrypi / $ cd /
pi@raspberrypi / $ cd /home/pi/Desktop/
pi@raspberrypi ~/Desktop $ cd ..
pi@raspberrypi ~ $ █
```

Changing between directories

The directory that you are in after you run cd is called the current working directory. Unless you specify, a directory bash will look for any commands that you run and any files that you are using in the current working directory. If the command is not in the current folder, bash will look in several other predefined folders for the command. These folders are specified in the PATH environment variable in bash.

pwd

Sometimes, when navigating the Linux filesystem, you might need to find out which directory you are in. You can do this using the pwd (print working directory) command.

```
pi@raspberrypi ~ $ pwd
/home/pi
pi@raspberrypi ~ $ cd /
pi@raspberrypi / $ pwd
/
pi@raspberrypi / $ ▮
```

The pwd command

cat

When you are working with files, sometimes it's very handy to quickly view the contents of a file. The cat command does exactly this. When you run the cat command followed by a filename, it will display the contents of that file on the screen.

```
pi@raspberrypi ~/Desktop $ cat minecraft-pi.desktop
[Desktop Entry]
Name=Minecraft Pi
Comment=Fun with Blocks
Exec=minecraft-pi
Icon=/usr/share/pixmaps/minecraft-pi.png
Terminal=false
Type=Application
Categories=Application;Game;
StartupNotify=true
pi@raspberrypi ~/Desktop $ ▮
```

The cat command

cat has several options that you can use to customize the format of the file on the screen. Some of the cat command's parameters are as follows:

Option	Description
-n	This shows line numbers in the file
-E	This adds $ at the end of every line so that you can see where it is

Remember that everything in Linux is a file. Using the cat command, you can read in data from the device on your Raspberry Pi, including its serial port and camera. By running cat /dev/video0 > video. record, you can record the video coming in from your camera.

head and tail

Another handy set of commands that you can use to see the contents of a file are head and tail. The head and tail commands go together and show the start of the end of a file. The head command is extremely useful if you want to see whether a big file is the file that you are looking for and it is too big to be shown using cat. The tail command is extremely handy if you want to look at the last few entries in a log file.

```
pi@raspberrypi ~/python_games $ head memorypuzzle.py
# Memory Puzzle
# By Al Sweigart al@inventwithpython.com
# http://inventwithpython.com/pygame
# Released under a "Simplified BSD" license

import random, pygame, sys
from pygame.locals import *

FPS = 30 # frames per second, the general speed of the program
WINDOWWIDTH = 640 # size of window's width in pixels
pi@raspberrypi ~/python_games $ tail memorypuzzle.py
def hasWon(revealedBoxes):
    # Returns True if all the boxes have been revealed, otherwise False
    for i in revealedBoxes:
        if False in i:
            return False # return False if any boxes are covered.
    return True


if __name__ == '__main__':
    main()pi@raspberrypi ~/python_games $ 
```

The head and tail commands

The head and tail commands have many different options that you can use in order to customize the output format of the file on the screen. The most important is the -n option. The -n option followed by a number will display *n* lines of the file. You can find the other options by running man head or man tail.

cp

cp is another important command in bash. cp copies a file or folder from one folder to another. By default, cp will overwrite a file in the destination folder if it already exists, so beware!

To use cp, you first need to specify the file or folder that you want to copy followed by the destination folder. If you select a directory, it will copy just this directory. If you want to make an exact copy of the directory, you need to use the -r command. The -r command recursively copies the folder.

Basically, what this command does is it makes an exact copy of the folder you are copying, so you will most likely want to use this option whenever you are copying a directory.

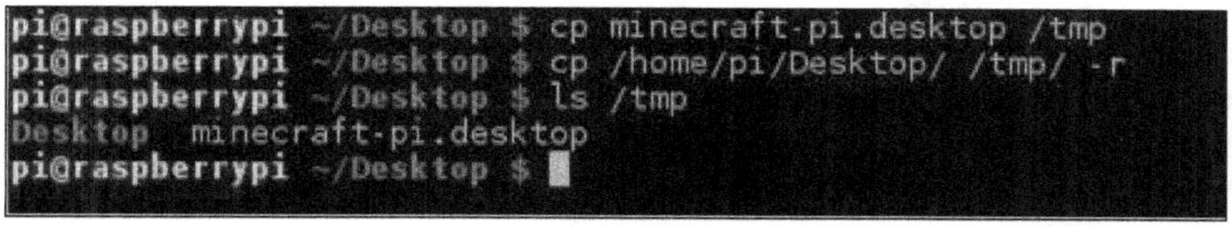

```
pi@raspberrypi ~/Desktop $ cp minecraft-pi.desktop /tmp
pi@raspberrypi ~/Desktop $ cp /home/pi/Desktop/ /tmp/ -r
pi@raspberrypi ~/Desktop $ ls /tmp
Desktop  minecraft-pi.desktop
pi@raspberrypi ~/Desktop $
```

Copying a file and a folder

The cp command has many different options that change how it copies a file or directory, as shown in the following table:

Option	Description
-r	This recursively copies a file or directory
-f	If an existing file in the destination directory can't be opened, this removes it and copies it again
-p	This preserves the owner and timestamp of the files that you are copying
-v	This indicates verbose mode, it shows the names of the files that are being copied

mv

Sometimes, you don't want to copy a file or directory, but instead you want to move it around. The mv command does exactly that. Its syntax is exactly the same as the syntax of cp. To move a file or folder, it is simply a matter of doing as shown in the following screenshot:

```
pi@raspberrypi ~/Desktop $ mv idle3.desktop /home/pi
pi@raspberrypi ~/Desktop $
```

Moving a file

Unlike cp, mv automatically moves the whole file or folder and it doesn't have an -r option. There are several other options available in mv, shown as follows:

Option	Description
-f	This overwrites any files and folders that are in the destination location
-u	This only moves the file if it is newer that the file in the destination folder

rm

Sometimes, a file or directory is no longer required and needs to be deleted. To do this, the rm command is used.

To delete a file or folder, simply run the rm command followed by the file or directory that you want to delete. Raspbian and most other Linux distributions don't contain any sort of recycle bin functionality. This means that when you delete something, it is permanently deleted.

Removing a file

There are very few things that you can do to destroy a Linux distribution. The sudo rm -rf / command is one of them. This command will start at the root directory and delete every file on your device, including any files on any removable and network drives attached to your Raspberry Pi. Needless to say, be very careful when using the -r and -f flags.

By default, when removing a directory, rm will stop if there are any files in the directory. To delete the directory, you will need to use the -f flag in order to force the deletion of the folder. Some of the rm command's parameters are as follows:

Option	Description
-f	This never prompts when deleting any files
-i	This prompts before deleting each and every file
-r	This recursively deletes the files and folders

mkdir

You will often need to create a new folder in order to keep your files organized. The purpose of using mkdir (make directory) is exactly that. To use mkdir, all you need to do is run mkdir followed by the name of the directory that you want to create.

```
pi@raspberrypi /tmp/work $ ls -ll
total 0
pi@raspberrypi /tmp/work $ mkdir demo
pi@raspberrypi /tmp/work $ ls -ll
total 4
drwxr-xr-x 2 pi pi 4096 Dec 13 17:06 demo
pi@raspberrypi /tmp/work $
```

Using mkdir

Once you have created the directory, it is immediately ready for use. You can use it to keep your files organized. Some of the `mkdir` parameters of are as follows:

Option	Description
-p	This creates any parent directories, if necessary—for example, `mkdir new/directory/with/parents -p`
-v	This displays a message for every directory that is created

touch

`touch` is a simple command that creates an empty file if a file doesn't exist. If the file exists, it updates the access time to when the command is run.

`touch` is often used when a file needs to exist. Some examples of this include creating empty log files. In order to use `touch`, run `touch` followed by the filename that you want to create or update the access time of.

```
pi@raspberrypi /tmp/work $ ls -ll
total 0
pi@raspberrypi /tmp/work $ touch new-file
pi@raspberrypi /tmp/work $ ls -ll
total 0
-rw-r--r-- 1 pi pi 0 Dec 13 17:00 new-file
pi@raspberrypi /tmp/work $
```

Using touch

adduser

Every file in Linux is owned by a user. This helps to keep everything secure. By default, everything in the `/home/pi` directory is owned by the Pi user. All users also belong to a group. You can allocate permissions depending on the owner and group of the user who owns the file.

You can add users to your Raspbian installation using the `adduser` command. To do this, run `adduser` followed by the username of the user that you want to create. Because `adduser` is a system command, you will need to add `sudo` before it.

```
pi@raspberrypi ~ $ sudo adduser newuser
Adding user `newuser' ...
Adding new group `newuser' (1004) ...
Adding new user `newuser' (1001) with group `newuser' ...
Creating home directory `/home/newuser' ...
Copying files from `/etc/skel' ...
Enter new UNIX password:
Retype new UNIX password:
passwd: password updated successfully
Changing the user information for newuser
Enter the new value, or press ENTER for the default
        Full Name []: New User
        Room Number []:
        Work Phone []:
        Home Phone []:
        Other []:
Is the information correct? [Y/n] y
pi@raspberrypi ~ $
```

Creating a user

You will be asked a couple of questions by `adduser`, including the username and password. If you don't want to provide your name or phone number, simply press the *Enter* key. The `adduser` command will also create a new group with the same name as your new user.

You can easily see which users you have in your Raspbian system by running the following command:

`cat /etc/passwd`

The `/etc/passwd` file contains all the users that are in Raspbian.

addgroup

Sometimes, you need to create a new group in order to organize your file permissions as required. To do this, use the `addgroup` command.

```
pi@raspberrypi ~ $ sudo addgroup newgroup
Adding group `newgroup' (GID 1005) ...
Done.
pi@raspberrypi ~ $
```

Creating a new group

The addgroup command is simple to use. All you need to do is to add the name of the group after the addgroup command.

The new group will be created along with a new ID. To see the groups that are there in Raspbian, run the following command:

```
cat /etc/group
```

passwd

As the system administrator of your very own Linux system, you have a lot of power. You can use this power to change users' passwords using the passwd command. There are a couple of different ways in which you can use passwd. One of them is to change your own password. Another way in which you can use passwd is to change the password of another user on your system.

Changing your password

To change your own password, run the passwd command as shown in the following screenshot:

```
pi@raspberrypi ~ $ passwd
Changing password for pi.
(current) UNIX password:
```

Changing your password

This will ask you to enter your current password. After you enter this, you will need to enter the new password twice.

Changing another user's password

Changing another user's password is just as easy as changing your password. To do this, add the username of the user after the passwd command. This command needs to be run as root, so add sudo before it.

```
pi@raspberrypi ~ $ sudo passwd newuser
Enter new UNIX password:
Retype new UNIX password:
```

Changing another user's password

This is really useful if you need to change someone else's password. By default, there is no root password set in Raspbian. To set it, run sudo passwd.

chown

As mentioned previously, Linux is a multiuser system and all the files have an owner. Sometimes, the owner needs to be changed. To do this, use the `chown` command. `chown` can change the user of a file or directory.

A good example of permissions in use is the Apache web server. All the configuration files in the `/etc/apache2` directory are owned by the Apache2 user, along with the files located in the `/var/www` directory where the website that Apache2 is serving.

Sometimes, when you add a file to this directory, you need to change the owner to be the Apache2 web server. If you don't do this, Apache2 won't be able to serve the file to anyone who wants to take a look at it.

`chown` needs several parameters. They are the new owner and the group of the file or directory that you want to change the owner of.

Changing the owner of all the files in Apache2's web root

The owner and group need to be separated by a (`:`). In the preceding example, the user and group are both Apache2.

There are several different options that you can add to the `chown` command, as follows:

Option	Description
-R	This changes the owner of all the files and folders in the folder recursively
-v	This displays a message for every file that is processed

Some of the chown command's parameters

chmod

The other part of a file's properties in Linux are its permissions. These permissions describe who can do what to files and directories. The following permissions are available:

Owner (o)	Read	Write	Execute
Group (g)	Read	Write	Execute
All users (a)	Read	Write	Execute

Linux file permissions

Each of these permissions is represented by a letter, as shown in the following table:

Read	r
Write	w
Execute	x

If you run the `ls -ll` command, you will be able to see what the permissions are for the file and directory that you are in:

```
pi@raspberrypi ~ $ ls -ll
total 28
drwxr-xr-x 2 pi pi 4096 Dec 13 15:55 Desktop
drwxr-xr-x 3 pi pi 4096 Nov 21 11:43 Documents
drwxr-xr-x 3 pi pi 4096 Nov 30 11:26 indiecity
-rw-r--r-- 1 pi pi 5781 Feb  3  2013 ocr_pi.png
drwxrwxr-x 2 pi pi 4096 Mar 10  2013 python_games
drwxr-xr-x 2 pi pi 4096 Nov 21 11:43 Scratch
pi@raspberrypi ~ $
```

The default permissions of the /home/pi directory

Permissions are grouped together in groups of three. The first three describe the users' permission for the file, the next three describe the group's permissions, and the last three describe permissions of all users.

The rw-r-r- permissions of the ocr_pi.png file are as follows:

	Permissions
Owner	Read and write
Group	Read
All users	Read

Permissions for ocr_pi.png

Octal representation of permissions

Permissions can also be described using an octal representation. This is a little more complicated but very flexible.

Octal notation	Permissions
0	No permissions
1	Execute
2	Write
3	Write and execute
4	Read
5	Read and execute
6	Read and write
7	Read, write, and execute

To describe the permissions of a file, simply work out what permissions you want to give. In the following example, we want the demo.txt file to have the following permissions:

	Permissions
Owner	Read and write
Group	Read only
All Users	No permissions

A demo of the permissions

To work out the permissions, we start with the owner and find the read and write permissions. We then do the same for the group and all users' permissions. These permissions work out as follows:

	Permissions
Owner	6
Group	4
All Users	0

Octal permissions for the file

These permissions are put together to be 640. The chmod command uses this representation to set the permissions of the file or folder.

```
lpi@raspberrypi ~/work $ ls -ll
total 0
-rw-r--r-- 1 pi pi 0 Dec 13 18:40 demo.txt
pi@raspberrypi ~/work $ chmod 640 ./demo.txt
pi@raspberrypi ~/work $ ls -ll
total 0
-rw-r----- 1 pi pi 0 Dec 13 18:40 demo.txt
pi@raspberrypi ~/work $ █
```

Changing the permissions of the demo.txt file

It is also possible to individually add and remove permissions from a file or folder. To do this, the user can use the notations described in the previous two tables.

We have the `demo.txt` file with the permissions as shown in the screenshot (*The default permissions of the /home/pi directory*) given earlier in this chapter. The permissions are as follows:

	Permissions
Owner	Read and write
Group	Read
All Users	No permissions

If we want to add the write permission to members of the same group, we do as shown in the following screenshot:

```
pi@raspberrypi ~/work $ chmod g+w ./demo.txt
pi@raspberrypi ~/work $ ls -ll
total 0
-rw-rw---- 1 pi pi 0 Dec 13 18:40 demo.txt
pi@raspberrypi ~/work $ █
```

Changing the permissions of the demo.txt file

The + symbol adds permissions and the – symbol removes permissions from files.

We can see that the file now has group permissions to read and write. The disadvantage of using this method is that you need to separately set the permissions of the file for the owner, group, and all users.

There are several other command-line parameters for chmod, as follows:

Parameter	Description
-R	This changes all the permissions for all the directories and files
-v	This displays a message for every file that is processed
-c	This only displays files that have their permissions changed

Command-line parameters for chmod

Redirection in bash

One of the more advanced features of bash are the redirection operators. These operators allow you to divert the input or output of a command to another command or file. While this sounds simple, it is an extremely powerful feature. There are several redirection operators built into bash, as shown here:

Operator	Description
|	This is a general-purpose command that chains similar to >
>	This redirects the output of a command to a file
<	This reads a file and passes it to the command
>>	This appends the output of the command to a file

Redirection operators

The | operator is a general-purpose command-changing tool. A simple example of this is to use it with cat and the program more. The more program is a simple program that lets you move backward and forward throughout a file on the screen in order to read it. The more command gets the data that you want to read from the cat command. The | operator connects two programs together.

```
# Memory Puzzle
# By Al Sweigart al@inventwithpython.com
# http://inventwithpython.com/pygame
# Released under a "Simplified BSD" license

import random, pygame, sys
from pygame.locals import *

FPS = 30 # frames per second, the general speed of the program
WINDOWWIDTH = 640 # size of window's width in pixels
WINDOWHEIGHT = 480 # size of windows' height in pixels
REVEALSPEED = 8 # speed boxes' sliding reveals and covers
BOXSIZE = 40 # size of box height & width in pixels
GAPSIZE = 10 # size of gap between boxes in pixels
BOARDWIDTH = 10 # number of columns of icons
BOARDHEIGHT = 7 # number of rows of icons
assert (BOARDWIDTH * BOARDHEIGHT) % 2 == 0, 'Board needs to have an even number of boxes for pair
s of matches.'
XMARGIN = int((WINDOWWIDTH - (BOARDWIDTH * (BOXSIZE + GAPSIZE))) / 2)
YMARGIN = int((WINDOWHEIGHT - (BOARDHEIGHT * (BOXSIZE + GAPSIZE))) / 2)

#            R    G    B
GRAY     = (100, 100, 100)
NAVYBLUE = ( 60,  60, 100)
WHITE    = (255, 255, 255)
RED      = (255,   0,   0)
GREEN    = (  0, 255,   0)
BLUE     = (  0,   0, 255)
YELLOW   = (255, 255,   0)
ORANGE   = (255, 128,   0)
PURPLE   = (255,   0, 255)
CYAN     = (  0, 255, 255)

BGCOLOR = NAVYBLUE
--More--
```

The more and cat commands connected using the | operator

> and >>

The > and >> operators are really powerful operators that take the data that is output by a program and write it to a file. The > operator replaces the file and the >> operator appends it to a file.

Remember that everything in Linux is a file, so you can use the > and >> operators to direct the output to a serial port or a printer.

```
pi@raspberrypi ~ $ ls -ll > dir.txt
pi@raspberrypi ~ $ cat dir.txt
total 32
drwxr-xr-x 2 pi pi 4096 Dec 13 15:55 Desktop
-rw-r--r-- 1 pi pi    0 Dec 14 07:21 dir.txt
drwxr-xr-x 3 pi pi 4096 Nov 21 11:43 Documents
drwxr-xr-x 3 pi pi 4096 Nov 30 11:26 indiecity
-rw-r--r-- 1 pi pi 5781 Feb  3  2013 ocr_pi.png
drwxrwxr-x 2 pi pi 4096 Mar 10  2013 python_games
drwxr-xr-x 2 pi pi 4096 Nov 21 11:43 Scratch
drwxr-xr-x 2 pi pi 4096 Dec 13 18:40 work
pi@raspberrypi ~ $
```

The > operator writes the result of an ls command to a file

<

The < operator is similar to the > operator, except that it reads the contents of a file and feeds it to a program. This can be used in a lot of ways and is in some ways similar to using <.

```
pi@raspberrypi ~ $ more < dir.txt
total 32
drwxr-xr-x 2 pi pi 4096 Dec 13 15:55 Desktop
-rw-r--r-- 1 pi pi    0 Dec 14 07:21 dir.txt
drwxr-xr-x 3 pi pi 4096 Nov 21 11:43 Documents
drwxr-xr-x 3 pi pi 4096 Nov 30 11:26 indiecity
-rw-r--r-- 1 pi pi 5781 Feb  3  2013 ocr_pi.png
drwxrwxr-x 2 pi pi 4096 Mar 10  2013 python_games
drwxr-xr-x 2 pi pi 4096 Nov 21 11:43 Scratch
drwxr-xr-x 2 pi pi 4096 Dec 13 18:40 work
pi@raspberrypi ~ $ 
```

Using the < operator to send the contents of dir.txt to the more application

Environmental variables

Another powerful feature of bash is the use of environmental variables. Environmental variables are values that are stored in memory and can be used to temporarily store information and settings. One example of this is the PATH variable. The PATH variable tells bash where to look for any programs if they aren't in the current directory.

All the current environmental variables set can be displayed using the printenv command. They are loaded into memory automatically when your Raspberry Pi boots up.

```
DESKTOP_SESSION=LXDE
PWD=/home/pi
LANG=en_GB.UTF-8
GDMSESSION=lightdm-xsession
_LXSESSION_PID=2669
SHLVL=1
HOME=/home/pi
XDG_CONFIG_HOME=/home/pi/.config
LOGNAME=pi
XDG_DATA_DIRS=/usr/local/share/:/usr/share/:/usr/share/gdm/:/var/lib/menu-xdg/
DBUS_SESSION_BUS_ADDRESS=unix:abstract=/tmp/dbus-wJZfMAFrcm,guid=4a9b54d2abdd57dfbab2f205548d3863
DISPLAY=:0.0
XDG_CURRENT_DESKTOP=LXDE
XAUTHORITY=/home/pi/.Xauthority
_=/usr/bin/printenv
pi@raspberrypi ~ $ 
```

Some of the environmental variables set up by default in Raspbian

You can define your own environmental variables easily in bash. By convention, in bash, all environmental variables are defined using capital letters.

To define an environmental variable, you can do as shown in the following screenshot:

```
pi@raspberrypi ~ $ MY_VARIABLE=a_value
pi@raspberrypi ~ $
```

Defining the MY_VARIABLE environmental value

Environmental variables can be used just as easily. To use an environmental variable, simply add $ before it.

```
pi@raspberrypi ~ $ echo $MY_VARIABLE
a_value
pi@raspberrypi ~ $
```

Using the MY_VARIABLE environmental value

Environmental variables are often used in shell scripts to store information and results.

 Do you know that a bug called Shellshock was discovered in 2014 in bash's handling of environmental variables? This bug allowed the execution of arbitrary commands and presented a huge risk to many of the web servers running on the Internet.

It is easy to add an environmental variable. To do this, you use the `export` command as follows:

```
export VARIABLE=value
```

An environmental variable's name can't contain a space and must contain capital letters.

Basic scripting

All the commands that you have seen so far are just single commands. The bash has the ability to execute multiple commands together in one go. Commands can be stored in a file called a shell script.

A shell script has its execute attribute set. It can then be run by simply changing into the directory that the script is in and typing its name.

These shell scripts can be run as normal program a on your Raspberry Pi.

Rebooting and shutting down your Raspberry Pi

You can reboot and shut down your Raspberry Pi using the built-in commands. To reboot your Raspberry Pi, all you need to do is run the `reboot` command.

Rebooting your Raspberry Pi

Sometimes, you will want to shut down your Raspberry Pi completely. To do this, you can use the `shutdown` command.

The `shutdown` command takes two different parameters: the first parameter is the type of shutdown that you want to do, and the second parameter is the time at which you want to do the shutdown.

Parameter	Description
-r	This reboots your Raspberry Pi.
-h	This powers off the system after the shutdown is complete. You will still need to disconnect the power to your Raspberry Pi when the shutdown is complete.
-k	This doesn't really shut down the system, it just sends a warning message.

The second parameter is normally the word `now`, which tells your Raspberry Pi that we want to shut down immediately.

Shutting down your Raspberry Pi!

The `halt` command can also be used if you want to shut down your Raspberry Pi. Simply run the following command:

halt

Your Raspberry Pi will immediately shut down.

Text editors

Sometimes, you might need to edit a file on your Raspberry Pi: perhaps to edit the `/etc/network/interfaces` file in order to reconfigure your Raspberry Pi network interfaces, or you might need a text editor to write a document.

Fortunately, there are several text editors installed with Raspbian. The most commonly used text editors are:

- nano
- vim

nano

Originally created in 1999 by Chris Allegretta, nano is the easiest text editor to use included on the Raspberry Pi.

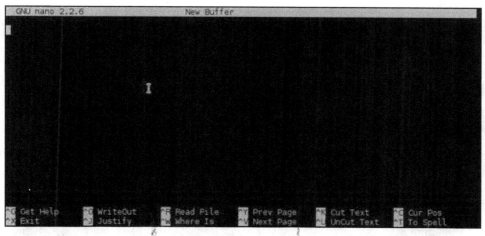

The nano text editor

To edit a file in nano, you simply need to start typing. Once you have made changes, you need to save them and exit. The commands that you see at the bottom of the screen can be accessed by pressing the *Ctrl* key on your keyboard followed by the letter.

1. For instance, to exit after you have made changes, press *Ctrl* + *x*.
2. You will then be asked whether you want to save these changes. To do so, press *y*.

Saving changes in nano

3. You now need to enter the filename that you want in order to save the file. Once you have done this, simply press *Enter* and your file will be saved.

Confirming the filename of the file you are saving

4. To load the file you have just saved, just run the nano command as shown in the following screenshot:

Selecting the filename that you want to save the file as

vim

The other text editor installed on your Raspberry Pi is the vi text editor. The vi editor was originally created for Unix-based operating systems by Bill Joy in 1976.

The name vi is derived from the shortened abbreviation of the word visual. The vi editor is one of the most widely used text editors in Linux.

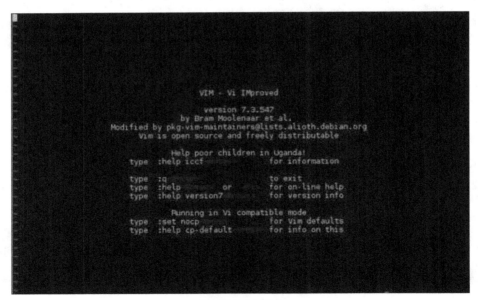

The vi text editor

The vim (improved vi) editor is a bit more complicated to use than nano. The vi editor is designed to stay out of your way, and as such, you won't see any menus or unnecessary information on the screen.

The vim editor has several different modes that you use to operate it. One of the modes is insert mode. When you are in insert mode, you can use vi like you would use the nano text editor, but here you simply type the text and use the arrow keys to navigate the file. To get into insert mode, press the *Insert* key or type a capital *I*.

The vi text editor in insert mode

In order to save the file, we need to enter in the command mode. To do this, press the *Esc* key followed by the *:* key. This will bring up a command prompt at the bottom of the vim window.

The vi text editor in command mode

There are many different commands available in vim, as follows:

Command	Description
w	This writes the file to disk
q	This is used to quit vim
dd	This deletes the current line of text
x	This deletes the character where the cursor is

These commands can be entered in Command Prompt, or when you are navigating the text and are not in insert mode.

An example of these commands is the wq command. This command saves and quits vim when you press *Enter*. You won't be asked whether you want to save your changes, as vim knows what you want, based on the command you give!

If you don't want to save your changes, simply enter the q! command.

There are many other text editors that can be installed onto your Raspberry Pi, such as geany.

Summary

In this chapter, you learned about the bash shell, file permissions, and many of bash's built-in commands. Remember that if you need to find out any more information, all that you need to do is add the man command in front of the command for which you want to find out more information. You will be able to find out as much information as you could ever need!

Remember, don't be scared to experiment with the different commands that are built into Raspbian. The worst thing that could happen is that you might need to image your SD card again.

7
Other Linux Distributions Based on Raspbian

Raspberry Pi is an extremely capable device that is within the reach of more people than ever. It is affordable enough for people to use for all sorts of different projects that weren't possible before. Some of these projects range from creating a media center for your TV to the autopilot functionality in an unmanned aerial vehicle.

Many of these projects are based on Raspbian, and many of these have become their own distribution. They are still Raspbian at heart, but they have been customized for a specific purpose, and you can use the skills that you have learned from this book to work with them. This chapter runs through some of the different distributions.

Raspbmc

Raspbmc (`http://www.raspbmc.com/`) is a Linux distribution based on Raspbian that lets you run XBMC (now called Kodi) on your Raspberry Pi. Kodi is an award-winning media player and entertainment hub designed to run on as many different devices as possible, including the Raspberry Pi.

Thanks to the Broadcom CPU and VideoCore IV graphics engine, the Raspberry Pi has more than enough power to handle media playback. This allows you to turn your Raspberry Pi into a powerful, extremely low-cost media center with low power consumption.

By installing Raspbmc on your Raspberry Pi, you can turn your Raspberry Pi into a fully-featured media center that can play movies and music on your TV. Kodi lets you use any smartphone or tablet with Wi-Fi as a remote control.

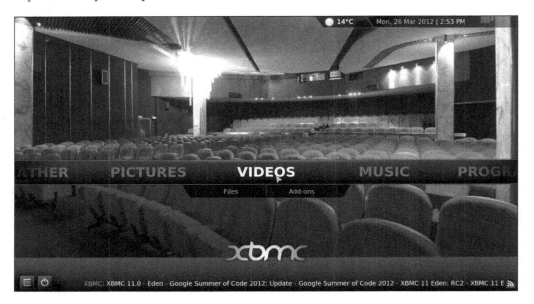

Volumio

Volumio (`http://volumio.org/`) is a free, open source Linux distribution based on Raspbian, designed to turn a Raspberry Pi into an audiophile music player. Volumio is designed to be easy to use. To quote the Volumio website, Volumio can be defined as follows:

> *"Volumio is designed to be simple. To sound amazing. To be what your music deserves."*

After installing Volumio onto your Raspberry Pi, you can control the music that you are playing using any smartphone or tablet with Wi-Fi.

The interesting thing about Volumio is that, as it has been designed for use by audiophiles (people who enjoy high-quality audio), it is designed to be able to use external **digital-to-analog converters (D/A)** to increase the quality of the sound being played. These D/A converters plug into your Raspberry Pi and work as a very high-quality sound card. The following image shows the Volumio web interface:

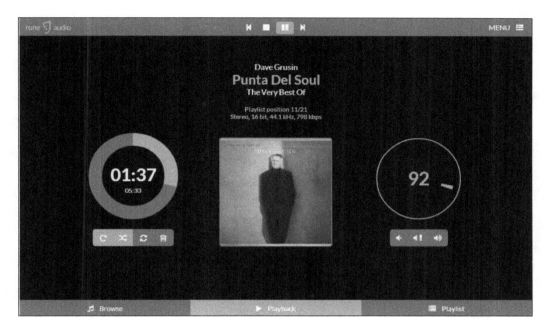

ThinBox

ThinBox (`http://www.jontylovell.net/index.php?page=30`) is a free, open source Linux distribution based on Raspbian, designed to turn you Raspberry Pi into a remote terminal client. ThinBox allows you to quickly and easily connect your Raspberry Pi to a Microsoft Windows based server or desktop.

Connections are easily set up using the built-in connection manager. ThinBox boots in less than 30 seconds to the desktop and has a simple, easy-to-use GUI application to set up connections. It is one of the easiest ways to use your Raspberry Pi to remotely access your systems from anywhere.

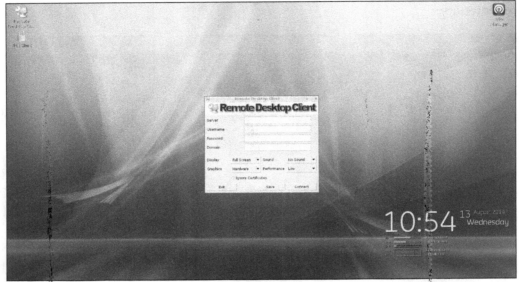

The desktop interface of ThinBox

PiPlay

PiPlay (http://pimame.org/) is another Linux distribution based on Raspbian, which is designed for gaming and emulating old gaming systems on your Raspberry Pi.

It is designed for users who have never used Linux or Raspberry Pi and is really easy to set up and use.

PiPlay emulates the following gaming systems:

- MAME—AdvanceMAME and MAME4ALL
- CPS I / CPS II—Final Burn Alpha
- NeoGeo—GnGeo
- Playstation—PCSX-ReARMed
- Genesis—DGen
- SNES—Snes9x

- NES — AdvMESS
- Gameboy — Gearboy
- Gameboy Advance — GPSP
- ScummVM
- Atari 2600 — Stella
- Cave story — NXEngine
- Commodore 64 — VICE

By installing PiPlay on your Raspberry Pi, you can play many old games that cannot be played any other way.

The PiPlay logo

Torberry

Torberry (`https://code.google.com/p/torberry/`) is a Raspbian-based Linux distribution for Raspberry Pi, designed to route all your Internet traffic through the Tor network.

According to the Tor website, Tor can be defined as follows:

> *"Tor is free software and an open network that helps you defend against traffic analysis, a form of network surveillance that threatens personal freedom and privacy, confidential business activities and relationships, and state security."*

Torberry is designed to be installed onto your Raspberry Pi and serve as a Tor transparent proxy that routes all your TCP and DNS traffic through the Tor network. This means that it is harder for someone to find your location.

The Tor logo

Kali

Kali (http://www.kali.org/) is a Linux distribution derived from Debian (as is Raspbian) designed for digital forensics and penetration testing.

Kali comes preinstalled with several software packages designed for testing the security of computer networks. These utilities allow the user to crack passwords, break into wireless networks, and perform port scans of someone's computer. Some of the tools included in Kali are shown in the following image:

Summary

In this chapter, you learned about several different operating systems that are based on Raspbian. These operating systems build on Raspbian to make your Raspberry Pi able to perform specialized tasks. These are only a small subset of some of the distributions available for the Raspberry Pi, and thanks to the popularity of the Raspberry Pi, more and more of these distributions will become available.

The skills that this book has taught you will help you with these distributions and allow you to make the most of them. Good luck!

References

Chapter 1, The Raspberry Pi and Raspbian

- http://en.wikipedia.org/wiki/File:Tux.svg#filelinks
- http://en.wikipedia.org/wiki/Linux_kernel
- https://kernel.org/category/about.html
- http://www.raspbian.org/FrontPage
- http://www.operating-system.org/betriebssystem/_english/bs-debian.htm
- http://lxde.org/lxde_desktop
- http://www.howtogeek.com/177213/linux-isnt-just-linux-8-pieces-of-software-that-make-up-linux-systems/

Chapter 2, Getting Started with Raspbian

- http://www.raspberrypi.org/documentation/installation/installing-images/README.md
- http://www.raspberrypi.org/help/quick-start-guide/
- http://en.wikipedia.org/wiki/Dd_(Unix)

Chapter 4, An Introduction to the Raspbian Desktop

- http://en.wikipedia.org/wiki/Dillo
- http://sonic-pi.net/

- http://wiki.lxde.org/en/LXTerminal
- http://en.wikipedia.org/wiki/IDLE_(Python)
- http://scratch.mit.edu/
- http://www.tldp.org/
- http://www.adeptus-mechanicus.com/codex/fslayout/fslayout.php
- http://en.wikipedia.org/wiki/Mathematica
- http://tones.wolfram.com/about/mathematica.html

Chapter 5, Installing Software on Raspbian

- http://www.raspbian.org/RaspbianFAQ
- http://en.wikipedia.org/wiki/Advanced_Packaging_Tool
- http://askubuntu.com/questions/309113/what-is-the-difference-between-dpkg-and-aptitude-apt-get
- http://en.wikipedia.org/wiki/Dpkg
- https://www.debian.org/doc/debian-policy/ch-archive.html
- http://w3techs.com/technologies/details/ws-apache/all/all
- http://en.wikipedia.org/wiki/LibreOffice

Chapter 6, The Console

- http://en.wikipedia.org/wiki/Bash_(Unix_shell)
- http://en.wikipedia.org/wiki/GNU_nano
- http://en.wikipedia.org/wiki/Vi

Chapter 7, Other Linux Distributions Based on Raspbian

- http://www.raspbmc.com/
- http://xbmc.org/about/
- http://sourceforge.net/blog/may-2014-staff-pick-project-of-the-month-piplay/
- http://pimame.org/
- https://www.torproject.org/
- http://en.wikipedia.org/wiki/Kali_Linux

Index

shutdown command
  -h parameter 118
  -k parameter 118
  -r parameter 118
  about 118
software
  IceDove 93
  IceWeasel 94
  installing, from source 88, 89
  LibreOffice 92
software installation
  from source, advantages 88
  from source, disadvantages 88
software installation methods,
    on Raspberry Pi
  about 76
  APT 77
  dpkg 76
Sonic Pi
  about 64
  URL 64
SSH
  enabling 43
Synaptic GUI Package Manager
  about 82
  packages, installing 83-85
  packages, searching 83, 84
  packages, uninstalling 86
  used, for installing updates 90, 91

T

tail command 104
text editors
  about 119
  nano 119
  vim 120
ThinBox
  about 125, 126
  URL 125
time zone
  selecting 39
Tor 127
Torberry
  about 127
  URL 127
touch command 107

U

unmount command 26
updates
  installing, with apt-get command 90
  installing, with Synaptic GUI Package
    Manager 90, 91

V

vim
  about 120, 121
  dd command 121
  insert mode 121
  q command 121
  w command 121
  x command 121
virtual desktops 50, 51
Volumio
  about 124
  URL 124

W

web browsers
  about 61
  Dillo 62
  Epiphany (web) 61
Wi-Fi dongle
  Raspberry Pi, connecting to 52
  URL 52
Wi-Fi network
  Raspberry Pi, connecting to 52
Win32 Disk Imager
  URL 19
Windows
  used, for writing image 19
wireless network
  connecting to 53, 54

X

Xfce
  file management 73
X.Org graphical server 14

Thank you for buying
Learning Raspbian

About Packt Publishing

Packt, pronounced 'packed', published its first book, *Mastering phpMyAdmin for Effective MySQL Management*, in April 2004, and subsequently continued to specialize in publishing highly focused books on specific technologies and solutions.

Our books and publications share the experiences of your fellow IT professionals in adapting and customizing today's systems, applications, and frameworks. Our solution-based books give you the knowledge and power to customize the software and technologies you're using to get the job done. Packt books are more specific and less general than the IT books you have seen in the past. Our unique business model allows us to bring you more focused information, giving you more of what you need to know, and less of what you don't.

Packt is a modern yet unique publishing company that focuses on producing quality, cutting-edge books for communities of developers, administrators, and newbies alike. For more information, please visit our website at www.packtpub.com.

About Packt Open Source

In 2010, Packt launched two new brands, Packt Open Source and Packt Enterprise, in order to continue its focus on specialization. This book is part of the Packt Open Source brand, home to books published on software built around open source licenses, and offering information to anybody from advanced developers to budding web designers. The Open Source brand also runs Packt's Open Source Royalty Scheme, by which Packt gives a royalty to each open source project about whose software a book is sold.

Writing for Packt

We welcome all inquiries from people who are interested in authoring. Book proposals should be sent to author@packtpub.com. If your book idea is still at an early stage and you would like to discuss it first before writing a formal book proposal, then please contact us; one of our commissioning editors will get in touch with you.

We're not just looking for published authors; if you have strong technical skills but no writing experience, our experienced editors can help you develop a writing career, or simply get some additional reward for your expertise.

Raspberry Pi Robotic Projects

ISBN: 978-1-84969-432-2   Paperback: 278 pages

Create amazing robotic projects on a shoestring budget

1. Make your projects talk and understand speech with Raspberry Pi.

2. Use standard webcam to make your projects see and enhance vision capabilities.

3. Full of simple, easy-to-understand instructions to bring your Raspberry Pi online for developing robotics projects.

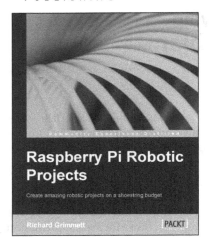

Raspberry Pi for Secret Agents

ISBN: 978-1-84969-578-7   Paperback: 152 pages

Turn your Raspberry Pi into your very own secret agent toolbox with this set of exciting projects!

1. Detect an intruder on camera and set off an alarm.

2. Listen in or record conversations from a distance.

3. Find out what the other computers on your network are up to.

4. Unleash your Raspberry Pi on the world.

Please check **www.PacktPub.com** for information on our titles

Raspberry Pi Cookbook for Python Programmers

ISBN: 978-1-84969-662-3   Paperback: 402 pages

Over 50 easy-to-comprehend tailor-made recipes to get the most out of the Raspberry Pi and unleash its huge potential using Python

1. Install your first operating system, share files over the network, and run programs remotely.

2. Unleash the hidden potential of the Raspberry Pi's powerful Video Core IV graphics processor with your own hardware accelerated 3D graphics.

3. Discover how to create your own electronic circuits to interact with the Raspberry Pi.

Raspberry Pi Networking Cookbook

ISBN: 978-1-84969-460-5   Paperback: 204 pages

An epic collection of practical and engaging recipes for the Raspberry Pi!

1. Learn how to install, administer, and maintain your Raspberry Pi.

2. Create a network fileserver for sharing documents, music, and videos.

3. Host a web portal, collaboration wiki, or even your own wireless access point.

4. Connect to your desktop remotely, with minimum hassle.

Please check **www.PacktPub.com** for information on our titles